1000 FACTS ON
MODERN
HISTORY

First published by Miles Kelly Publishing Ltd
Bardfield Centre, Great Bardfield
Essex, CM7 4SL

2 4 6 8 10 9 7 5 3 1

Editor
Belinda Gallagher

Assistant Editor
Mark Darling

Art Director
Clare Sleven

Designer
Debbie Meekcoms

Picture Research
Liberty Newton

British Library Cataloguing-in-Publication Data
A catalogue record for this book is available from the British Library

ISBN 1-84236-054-X

Printed in Hong Kong

www.mileskelly.net
info@mileskelly.net

1000 FACTS ON MODERN HISTORY

John Farndon
Consultant Richard Tames

Miles Kelly
PUBLISHING

Contents

Key

 People

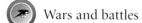 Wars and battles

 Europe

 The Americas

 Events

 The World

Contents

Contents

The Norman invasion

- **On 5 January 1066,** the English king Edward the Confessor died. As he died, he named as his successor Harold Godwinson – the powerful earl of the kingdom of Wessex.

- **Harold's claim** to the English throne was challenged by William, the duke of Normandy in France, who claimed that Edward had already promised him the throne.

▲ *William's troops rapidly seized control of England. This was the last time the country was conquered by a foreign power.*

- **Harold's claim** was also challenged by Harold Hardraade (the Ruthless), the king of Norway.

- **In autumn 1066,** Hardraade invaded northern England with Harold Godwinson's brother Tostig. His army was routed by Harold's at Stamford Bridge on 25 September.

- **On 27 Sept,** William's Norman army of 7000 crossed from France and landed at Pevensey in S. England.

- **Harold marched** his army south to meet the Normans, walking over 300 km to London in just five days.

▲ *The Normans commemorated their victory at the Battle of Hastings with a famous tapestry, made in England, now in Bayeux in France.*

- **Harold's tired army** met the Normans at Hastings in Sussex on the 14th of October, and took a stand by the Hoar Apple Tree on Caldbec Hill.

- **Harold's army** was mauled by William's archers, but axe-wielding English house-carles (infantry) put the Norman cavalry to flight. Harold was then killed – perhaps by an arrow. The English fought on for a while before fleeing.

- **After the battle** William moved on London, where he was crowned king in Westminster Abbey on 25 December.

- **Within** a few years, the Normans had conquered England.

The great khans

- **The Mongols** were nomads who lived in yurts (huts made of felt) in central Asia, as many still do.

- **In 1180,** a 13-year-old Mongol boy called Temujin was made khan (chief) of his tribe. He soon became a great leader, and in 1206 he was hailed as Genghis Khan (Chief of all Men).

- **Genghis Khan** was a brilliant and ruthless soldier. His armies terrified their enemies, and butchered anyone they met.

- **Genghis's horse archers** could kill at 180 m while riding at full gallop. They once rode 440 km in just three days.

- **In just four years (1210-14),** Genghis Khan conquered northern China, much of India and Persia. His empire stretched right through Asia from Korea to the Caspian Sea.

▼ *Genghis Khan was a man of incredible physical strength and willpower. He could be tyrannical and cruel, yet philosophers would travel from far away to talk with him about religion.*

- **After Genghis Khan** died, his son Ogodai ravaged Armenia, Hungary and Poland.

- **Genghis Khan's grandson** – Kublai Khan – conquered the rest of China in 1265 and made himself the first of a line of Mongol emperors of China called Yuans. The Yuans lasted until 1368.

- **Kublai's** rule in China was harsh, but he was greatly admired by the Venetian traveller, Marco Polo.

- **Kublai Khan** created a grand new capital called Ta-tu ('the Great Capital') – now Beijing.

- **Kublai Khan** adopted Chinese ways of government and ruled with such efficiency that China became very rich.

◄ *A man of vision, energy, and a certain ruthlessness, Kublai Khan encouraged the arts and sciences, rebuilt Beijing and made Buddhism the state religion – suppressing Taoism in the process. First emperor of the Yuan dynasty, he gave China a strong separate identity and led a glittering court that was famed far and wide.*

The Aztecs

- **In the 1200s,** a tribe called the Aztecs found that the only place to settle in crowded Mexico was on a lake.

- **By 1325,** the Aztecs were powerful and their lake home Tenochtitlán was a splendid city with canals and temples.

- **Aztec farmers** walked or rowed dugout canoes for hours to markets in cities like Tlateloco to sell farm produce in return for cocoa beans, which they used as money.

- **In Aztec society,** a powerful priest-king plus priests and nobles ruled ordinary folk and slaves with an iron hand.

- **The Aztecs** built vast pyramids topped by temples where priests made bloody human sacrifices on a huge scale.

- **The Aztecs** made human sacrifices because they believed that this gave their god Huitzilopochtli the strength to fight off the night and bring the morning.

- **In a special, sacred ball game** teams hit a rubber ball through a small ring in an I-shaped court – using their hips, knees and elbows. This very violent game caused serious injury, even death.

- **One of the ways** we know about the Aztecs is from folding books of picture-writing called codices, written by Aztec scribes. The most famous is the *Codex Mendoza*.

- **By 1521,** the Aztec Empire was finished. Spanish treasure-seekers led by Hernando Cortés defeated Montezuma II, the Aztec emperor, and plundered the Aztecs' land and riches.

▲ *This vast Pyramid of the Sun, built as four huge steps, is part of the ruined Aztec city of Teotihuacán. Archaeologists have found a human skeleton at the corner of each step – buried alive as part of the Aztecs' rituals of human sacrifice.*

FASCINATING FACT
Every year Tenochtitlán took in 9000 tonnes of corn, beans and seeds in taxes.

The Magna Carta

- **John I** was king of England from 1199 to 1216. He was one of the most unpopular kings in history.

- **John was nicknamed** 'Lackland' by his father Henry II because, unlike his older brothers Richard and Geoffrey, he did not inherit land to provide him with an income.

- **John was hated** for his cruelty, for the demands he put on his barons for tax and military service and for trying to seize the crown while his popular brother King Richard the Lionheart was Crusading.

- **On 15 June 1215,** rebellious barons compelled John to meet them at Runnymede on the Thames and agree to their demands by sealing the Magna Carta ('Great Charter').

- **Ordinary people** gained little at the time from the Magna Carta but it is now seen as the world's first bill of rights and the start of fair government in England.

- **The Magna Carta** showed that even the king had to obey the law.

- **Magna Carta** contained 63 clauses, most relating to feudal customs.

- **Clause 39** gave every free man the right to a fair trial. Clause 40 gave everyone the right to instant justice.

- **Some parts of** the Magna Carta dealt with weights and measures, foreign merchants and catching fish.

- **John** got the pope to annul the document three days later, but it was reissued in 1225, after John's death.

▼ *The barons compelled King John to put his seal (wax stamp) on the Magna Carta at Runnymede in 1215.*

Saladin

- **Saladin** was perhaps the greatest Muslim (Islamic) leader of the Middle Ages. To his people he was a saintly hero. Even his Christian enemies were awed by his honour and bravery.

- **Saladin is famed** as a brilliant soldier, but he was also deeply religious. He built many schools, mosques and canals.

- **Saladin was a Kurd,** born in Tekrit, now in Iraq, in 1137, but he was brought up in Syria.

- **He became** a soldier at the age of 14. Right from the start he had an intense belief in the idea of *jihad* – the holy war to defend the Islamic religion.

- **Saladin's leadership** brought him to prominence and in 1169 he was effectively made sultan (ruler) of Egypt.

- **By diplomacy and conquest,** he united the Muslim countries – torn apart by rivalries for the 88 years since the Crusaders captured Jerusalem in 1099.

- **In 1187,** with Islam united, Saladin was able to turn his attentions to driving the Crusaders out of the Near East.

◄ *Saladin must have been a single-minded and ambitious man, but those who met him said he was the most humble, moral and generous of rulers. Strangely, he died virtually penniless.*

- **On 4 July 1187** Saladin routed the Crusaders at Hattin in Palestine. This victory was so devastating to the Crusaders that within three months the Muslims had recaptured almost every bit of land they had lost.

- **Shocked by the fall** of Jerusalem, the Christian countries threw themselves into their last major Crusade, led in part by the great Richard the Lionheart.

- **Such was Saladin's** leadership that the Muslims fought off the Crusaders' onslaught. Eventually, Richard and Saladin met up and, in a spirit of mutual admiration, drew up a truce that ended the Crusades.

▶ *Here, a knight and his personal page prepare to do battle in the Crusades. These were holy wars fought between 1099 and 1291, in order to recapture Christian holy sites from Muslims.*

Bannockburn

- **In 1286, King Alexander III** of Scotland died. His grand-daughter – Margaret, 'Maid of Norway' – died four years later. Their deaths left no obvious successor to the Scottish throne.

- **The Scottish lords** agreed to the suggestion of English king Edward I that he should decide between the 13 rival claimants, including John de Balliol and Robert Bruce.

- **Edward I** marched into Scotland, imprisoned the leading claimant John de Balliol and declared himself king. Some of Balliol's rivals, such as Robert, supported Edward.

- **The Scottish lords** did not react, but a small landowner called William Wallace began a heroic fight. With a band of just 30 men, he attacked Lanark, took the garrison and killed the English sheriff. Commoners flocked to his aid.

- **On 4 May 1297,** Wallace's small rebel army scored a stunning victory over the English at Stirling. He drove the English from Scotland and marched on into England. But the Scottish lords still gave him no support.

  - **Wallace** was captured by the English in 1305. He was hanged, drawn (disembowelled) and quartered (cut in four pieces). His head was stuck on a pole on London Bridge.

  - **Wallace's** heroism inspired Robert Bruce to lead a rebellion that finally included the Scottish lords.

◀ *The story goes that, while in hiding, Robert Bruce was inspired to go on fighting after seeing a spider struggle up its thread again and again – and eventually succeed.*

- **Letting his enemies** think he was dead, Robert launched a campaign from Ireland in 1306. Within two years he had cleared the English from Scotland again.

- **Robert scored** a last decisive victory over the English under Edward II at Bannockburn on 23-24 June 1314. With this victory, the Scots regained their independence.

▼ *Scottish hero Robert Bruce freed the Scots from English control at the Battle of Bannockburn, in 1314.*

FASCINATING FACT
At Bannockburn, just 5000 Scots may have routed an English army of 23,000.

African empires

▶ *The splendid ancient city of Great Zimbabwe, now in ruins, flourished in southern Africa and gave its name to modern Zimbabwe. At its height, the city's population was up to 18,000.*

- **From 1000 to 1500,** the interaction of black, Bantu-speaking Africans with Arab Muslims shaped African history.

- **In East Africa,** Bantu people and Arabs mixed to create the culture and language called Swahili.

- **Trade in gold and ivory** created thriving ports down the East African coast – such as Zanzibar and Kilwa.

- **Inland**, the city of Great Zimbabwe (the name means 'house of stone') flourished within its huge granite walls. It is now a ruin, but in the 1400s, gold made this city the heart of the Monomatapa Empire.

- **Further inland,** by the lakes of Uganda, were the extraordinary grass palaces of the Bugandan kings.

- **In West Africa,** trade across the Sahara made kingdoms like Ghana flourish. Two great empires grew up – first Mali (1240-1500) and then Songhai, which peaked in the 1500s.

- **The Mali** Empire centred on the city of Timbuktu.

- **Timbuktu's** glory began in 1324, when King Mansa Musa went on a grand trip to Mecca with camels laden with gold and brought back the best scholars and architects.

▲ *A bust made by the Edo people of Benin, Africa's greatest city during the 1600s.*

- **Timbuktu** means 'mother with a large navel', after an old woman said to have first settled here. But from 1324 to 1591 Timbuktu was a splendid city with what may have been the world's biggest university, catering for up to 25,000 students.

- **The Songhai Empire** in the 1400s stretched right across West Africa from what is now Nigeria to Gambia. It reached its peak under Sunni Ali (1464-92), who conquered Timbuktu, and his son Askia the Great (1493-1528).

Serfs and lords

- **When the Roman** Empire collapsed, a new way of ordering society, called the feudal system, emerged.

- **In the feudal system,** a king or overlord gave a lord a fief (a grant of land). In return, the lord swore to train and fight for the king as a knight (horse warrior). Land was the security because it could not be moved. Any lord who got a fief was called his king's vassal.

- **In 732, Charles Martel,** ruler of the Franks (now France) drove back the invading Muslims at the Battle of Tours. But he was worried he might not beat the brilliant Muslim horsemen if they came back. So he developed one of the first feudal systems.

- **There were** different levels in the feudal system. The count of Champagne had 2017 vassal knights, but he himself was vassal to ten overlords, including the king of France.

- **Only noblemen** could join the feudal system, but it soon took over most land in Europe, as kings tied their subjects by grants of land.

- **There was a saying,** 'No land without a lord; and no lord without a land'.

- **With so much land** in fiefs, most peasants were serfs, legally bound to their lords by the 'manorial' system, which centred on a lord's manor or castle.

▶ *Most people in medieval Europe were poor serfs tied to their lord. They lived in basic huts clustered round the lord's manor house and scraped a meagre living.*

- **Serfs** were given small plots of land to live off in return for working their lord's land.

- **Serfs** could not be evicted, but had few rights. They could not leave the village, marry or sell their possessions without their lord's permission.

- **The feudal and manorial systems** reached their peak in the 1100s but then began to decline.

▲ In return for basic food and housing, serfs worked their lords' lands and had virtually no personal freedom. In the Middle Ages, most people in Europe worked on the land. Almost everything they owned, from food and clothing to land and animals – belonged to the local lord.

Crusades

- **In the 11th century,** western Christian countries were threatened by the Muslim Seljuk Turks. In 1095, they were just outside Constantinople, capital of the Byzantine Empire and the centre of Christianity in the east. The emperor Alexander Comnenus appealed to the pope, Urban II, for help.

- **Urban II** held a meeting of church leaders at Clermont in France. He called for warriors to drive back the Turks and reclaim the Holy Land. This became a holy pilgrimage or Crusade. The word 'Crusade' comes from the Latin *crux*, meaning 'cross'.

- **Before the armies** could set out, 50,000 peasants began marching from western Europe on their own 'People's Crusade' to free the Holy Land. They had been stirred by tales of Turkish atrocities, spread by a preacher called Peter the Hermit. Many peasants died or got lost on the way; the rest were killed by Turks.

- **In 1096,** armies of well-trained French and Norman knights set out on the First Crusade. At Constantinople, they joined up with the Byzantines. Despite quarrelling on the way, they captured Jerusalem in 1099 and then set about massacring Jews and Turks mercilessly.

◄ *When the Crusader knights set out to fight for control of Jerusalem, in the Holy Land, they went with different motives. Some were courageous men with a deep sense of honour and a holy purpose. Others were adventurers, out for personal gain or glory. This Crusader wears the famous uniform of the Knights Templars.*

- **After capturing** Jerusalem, the Crusaders divided the Holy Land into four parts or Counties, together known as Outremer (said 'oot-rer-mare'), which meant 'land beyond the seas'. The Crusaders ruled Outremer for 200 years and built great castles like Krak des Chevaliers in Syria.

- **Two bands of soldier-monks** formed to protect pilgrims journeying to the Holy Land – the Knights Hospitallers of St John and the Knights Templars. The Hospitallers wore black with a white cross. The Templars wore a red cross on white, which became the symbol of all Crusaders.

- **By 1144,** Crusader control in Outremer weakened, and the Turks advanced. King Louis VII of France and King Conrad of Germany launched a Second Crusade. But by 1187, Saladin had retaken most of Outremer.

- **In 1190,** the three most powerful men in Europe – Richard I of England, Philip II of France and Frederick Barbarossa (Holy Roman Emperor) – set off on the Third Crusade. Barbarossa died on the way and Philip II gave up. Only Richard went on, and secured a truce with Saladin.

- **In 1212,** thousands of children set off on a Children's Crusade to take back Jerusalem, led by French farm boy Stephen of Cloyes. Sadly, most were lured on to ships in Marseilles and sold into slavery or prostitution.

> ...FASCINATING FACT...
> The most famous Crusader was King Richard I of
> England, known as the Lionheart for his bravery.

Marco Polo

- **Marco Polo** was a famous Italian traveller. Born c.1254 in Venice, he spent many years in the court of Kublai Khan, emperor of China.

  - **In the 1200s,** most of Europe knew China only as the romantic land of 'Cathay'. But Marco's father Niccolo and uncle Maffeo were well-travelled merchants who had already been there.

  - **In 1271,** Niccolo and Maffeo invited 17-year-old Marco to come with them to Cathay again.

  - **The Polos took four years** to reach China, travelling on foot and horse along the 'Silk Road' – a route north of the Himalayan mountains. The Silk Road was the way merchants brought silk from China to Europe.

  - **Kublai Khan** welcomed the Polos. Marco had a gift for languages and became one of the Khan's diplomats.

◄ *While in China, Marco Polo is said to have served as governor of Yangzhou.*

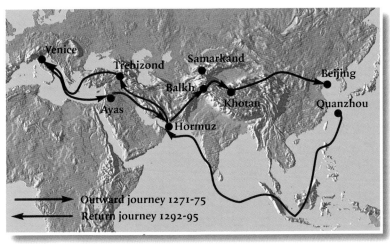

▲ *Marco Polo was one of the few Europeans to journey all the way to China and back in the Middle Ages.*

- **After 17 years,** the Polos decided to come back – but the Khan would only let them go if they took with them a princess who was to be wed to the Khan's grand-nephew in Persia.

- **The Polos** arrived back in Venice in 1295, laden with jewels, silks and spices.

- **Marco Polo** later wrote an account of his time in China while a prisoner of war in Genoa, dictating it to a man called Rustichello.

- **Marco's** tales were so fantastic that some called the book *Il milione* ('The million lies'). Some experts now think that he reported the truth as he saw it. Others think he just recycled other travellers' tales.

- **Christopher Columbus** was just one of many people inspired by Marco Polo's accounts.

The Black Death

- **The Black Death** was the terrible epidemic of bubonic plague and pneumonia that ravaged Europe between 1347 and 1351.

- **The Black Death** of the 1300s was perhaps the worst disaster ever to have struck humanity.

▲ *The Plague brought death so close to people that they began to think of it as a real person.*

- **Worldwide,** the Black Death killed 40 million people.

- **The Black Death** killed 25 million people in Europe.

- **The disease** probably started in China. It was transmitted to Europeans when a Kipchak (Mongol) raiding party catapulted infected corpses into a Genoese trading centre in the Crimea.

- **The plague reached Genoa** in 1347 and spread west and north, reaching London and Paris in 1348.

- **The plague was** carried first by rat fleas that could also live on humans. It then changed to pneumonic plague, which was spread through coughs and sneezes.

- **After the Black Death,** fields were littered with bodies. Houses, villages and towns stood silent and empty.

- **Afterwards** there was such a shortage of labour that wages soared and many serfs gained their freedom.

▲ *Plague returned several times over the centuries, including London's Great Plague of 1665. Houses struck by this highly infectious scourge were traditionally marked with a cross.*

. . . **FASCINATING FACT** . . .
The Black Death killed more than one in
every four Europeans in just four years.

The Hundred Years' War

- **The Hundred Years' War** was a long war between France and England, lasting from 1337 to 1453.

- **The war** was caused by disputes over Guyenne (English land in southwest France), English claims to the French throne, French support for the Scots and French efforts to block the English wool trade in Belgium.

- **1337:** French king Philip VI tried to take over Guyenne. English king Edward III, whose mother was sister to three French kings, retaliated by claiming the French throne.

- **1340:** Edward won a great naval battle off Sluis, Belgium.

- **1346:** Edward III's archers – outnumbered 3 to 1 – routed the greatest French knights at Crécy with their great 2-m-long yew bows, and so hastened the end of knighthood.

- **1347:** Edward III took the French port of Calais.

- **1356:** Edward III's son, the Black Prince, won a great victory over the French at Poitiers.

- **1415:** the last great English victory was Henry V's at Agincourt; 6000 English beat a French army of 30,000.

- **The English** won most battles, but the French won the war because they had three times the resources.

◀ *The greatest knight of the war was Edward the Black Prince (1330-76), hero of the Battles of Crécy, Poitiers and Navarette.*

▲ In the Battle of Agincourt (1415),
the French failed to learn lessons
from previous defeats and
Henry V won a glorious victory.

> ### FASCINATING FACT
> The tide turned for the French in 1429, when
> Joan of Arc led them to victory at Orléans.

The Hanseatic League

- **By the 1400s,** the feudal system of knights fighting part-time in exchange for land was outmoded. Kings now relied on full-time armies.

- **Kings turned** to newly rich merchants to pay for their armies, so merchants gained power. The Italians invented banks to give loans.

- **From the 1300s,** many serfs gained freedom and became prosperous 'yeoman' farmers. They needed merchants to sell their produce.

- **After the Crusades,** silks, spices and riches from the east were traded in the Mediterranean for cloth, hides and iron. In northern Europe, the wool trade thrived.

- **Trading towns** began to grow across western Europe in the 1300s and 1400s – Antwerp, Flanders, Bruges, Bristol, Norwich, York, Florence, Venice, Milan and many others.

- **Trading towns** grew powerful. In England, many became boroughs with charters giving them some self-rule.

- **Merchants and traders** organized guilds (like trade unions) to defend their rights.

- **In 1241,** the German ports of Hamburg and Lübeck set up a *hanse* (guild) to protect merchants against pirates. The *hanse* grew into a very powerful Hanseatic League that monopolized trade around the Baltic Sea.

- **The Hanseatic League** set up special areas in cities across north Europe and controlled most trading routes. The League also put financial pressure on kings and lords to keep them at peace, and not to disrupt trade.

- **Hanseatic merchants** brought raw materials, spices and silks from eastern Europe and traded them for cloth, linen, silverware and woollen clothes from the west.

▶ *Riches from the Hanseatic traders helped Hamburg build a great cathedral in the Middle Ages.*

The Great Schism

- **In the Middle Ages,** kings and lords battled with the Church over who had the right to run people's lives.

- **The Church** was all-powerful but riddled with corruption. Men like John Wycliffe (1320-84) began to argue that it had too much power. He was supported by English kings.

- **Between 1214-94,** scholars called 'scholastics', such as Roger Bacon, tried to use reason to understand Christian ideas.

- **The French scholar** Peter Abelard argued that we should ask questions. 'By doubting, we come to inquiry, and by inquiry we come to truth.'

- **Churchmen** like Bernard of Clairvaux opposed scholastics: 'the faith of the righteous believes; it does not dispute.'

- **In 1302, Pope Boniface VIII** issued a decree called the *Unum sanctum*, stating that everyone was subject to him.

- **French king** Philip IV said Boniface was trying to claim authority over the French king and French people.

- **In 1309,** Pope Clement V moved from Rome to Avignon in France. This became home to a series of French popes, until Pope Gregory XI went back to Rome in 1377.

- **When Gregory XI** died in 1378, there was a Great Schism (split) in the Church. Some claimed Italian Urban VI as pope. Others supported Robert from Switzerland. Urban stayed in Rome and Robert went back to Avignon. In 1409, some church leaders declared a third pope.

- **In 1417,** the Great Schism was ended when a council of all Church leaders elected Martin V as pope in Rome. But the dispute had weakened the Church's authority fatally.

▲ *The impressive Palace of the Popes in Avignon, southern France, was built between 1314 and 1370. It was the home of the French popes for 100 years during the time of the Great Schism.*

The Ottoman wars

- **In 1281,** a new power began to emerge in Turkey from a tiny state called Sögüt, led by a ruler called Osman.

- **Over 200 years** a huge Muslim empire was built up, called the Ottoman Empire after Osman's descendants. It stretched from the Euphrates River on the borders of Persia to the Danube in Hungary.

- **In 1453,** Christian Constantinople fell to the Ottoman Turks and became their capital, Istanbul.

- **For centuries,** the Christian countries of Europe were threatened by Turkish expansion.

▲ *The Barbarossa brothers, Aruj and Khir, were Turkish pirates who helped to bring Tunisia and Algeria into the Ottoman Empire.*

- **Ottoman power** peaked in the 1520s under Suleiman, known as Qanuni ('law-giver') by Turks and 'the Magnificent' by Europeans because of his splendid court.

- **Suleiman** took all Hungary and attacked Vienna in 1529.

- **In 1522,** Suleiman took the island of Rhodes from his sworn enemies, the Knights of St John, who moved to Malta and built the fort of Valetta.

- **In the 1520s,** the Turkish pirate Khayr or Barbarossa (Spanish for Redbeard) took most of North Africa and became an Ottoman admiral. Algeria and the Barbary coast (North Africa) became a feared base for pirates for 300 years.

- **In 1565,** Suleiman attacked the Knights of St John in Valetta, but they survived.

- **When the Turks** attacked Cyprus in 1571, Venetian, Spanish and Papal fleets combined to crush them at the crucial battle of Lepanto in Greece. Turkish power declined after this.

▶ *Lepanto was the last great battle between fleets of galleys – warships powered by huge banks of oarsmen.*

The Wars of the Roses

- **The Wars of the Roses** were a series of civil wars fought in England in the 1400s as two branches of the Plantagenet family fought for the English throne.

- **On one side** was the house of York, with a white rose as its emblem. On the other was the house of Lancaster, with a red rose as its emblem.

- **The wars began** when Lancastrian king Henry VI became insane in 1453. With the country in chaos, Warwick the 'kingmaker' set up Richard, duke of York as Protector in Henry's place.

- **In 1455, Henry VI** seemed to recover and war broke out between Lancastrians and Yorkists.

  - **Richard** was killed at the Battle of Wakefield in 1460, but Henry VI became insane again.

  - **A crushing Yorkist victory** at Towton, near York, in 1461, put Richard's son on the throne as Edward IV.

  - **Edward IV** made enemies of his brothers Clarence and Warwick, who invaded England from France in 1470 with Henry VI's queen Margaret of Anjou and drove Edward out.

▲ *The white – and red – roses were emblems of the rival houses of York and Lancaster. When Henry VII wed Elizabeth of York, he combined the two to make the Tudor rose.*

- **Henry VI** was brought back for seven months before Edward's Yorkists defeated the Lancastrians at Barnet and Tewkesbury. Henry VI was murdered.

- **When Edward IV** died in 1483, his son Edward V was still a boy. When young, Edward and his brother vanished – probably murdered in the Tower of London – and their uncle Richard III seized the throne.

- **Richard III** made enemies among the Yorkists, who sided with Lancastrian Henry Tudor. Richard III was killed at Bosworth Field on 22 August 1485. Henry Tudor became Henry VII and married Elizabeth of York to end the wars.

▲ *Richard was a harsh man, but not the evil monster portrayed in Shakespeare's play,* Richard III.

Monasteries

- **Monasteries** played a key role in medieval life in Europe, reaching a peak in the 1200s.

- **The most famous monastery** was Cluny in France, but there were thousands of others in France and England.

- **Most monasteries** had a church called an abbey, some of which are among the greatest medieval buildings.

- **Monasteries** were the places where the poor went for welfare and they were also the only hospitals.

- **Monasteries** were places for scholars to study. They were the only libraries. Most great works of medieval art, literature and scholarship came from monasteries.

▲ *Like most English monasteries, the great 12th-century Cistercian monastery at Tintern in Wales was destroyed by Henry VIII.*

- **Monasteries** were great landowners with immense power and wealth. In England, monasteries owned a third of the land and a quarter of the country's wealth. They were also Europe's biggest single employers.

- **Many monasteries** oppressed the poor by taking over land and taking a heavy toll in tithes (church taxes).

- **Many monasteries** became notorious for the indulgence of their monks in fine food and high living.

- **New orders** of monks tried every now and then to go back to a simpler life, like the Cistercians from Citeaux in France and the Premonstratensians from Laon in France.

▲ *Franciscan friars. The Franciscan order was founded by St Francis of Assisi in the early 1200s.*

- **Cistercians** founded monasteries in barren places like Fountains in Yorkshire. But even they grew rich and lazy.

China

- **After almost a century** of chaos, the Song dynasty (family) of emperors came to power in China in AD 960. The Songs ruled until the early 1200s, when the Mongol Khans invaded and their time is perhaps the golden age of Chinese civilization.

- **The Song rulers** renounced the warlike policies that had kept China in strife, and brought peace by paying tribute money to the barbarian peoples in the north. They had a huge army, but this was partly to give jobs to hundreds of thousands of poor Chinese.

- **The Song slowly got rid** of soldiers from government and replaced them with civil servants.

- **In earlier times**, only aristocrats tended to hold key posts in government, but under the Song, anyone could enter for the civil service exams. Competition to do well in the exams was intense, and the main yearly exams became major events in the calendar.

◄ *When the Mongol Khans seized China from the Song, they made a new capital in the north at Beijing. At its centre lies a walled area containing the emperor's palaces. It is called the Forbidden City because only the emperor and his servants could enter it.*

- **The civil service exams** stressed not practical skills but the study of literature and the classic works of the thinker Confucius. So the Song civil service was full of learned, cultured men, known in the west as mandarins. Ou Yang-hsiu was a typical mandarin – statesman, historian, poet, philosopher, wine and music connoisseur and brilliant player of the chess-like game *wei-ch'i*.

- **Under the Song,** the Chinese population soared, trade prospered and all kinds of advances were made in science and technology – from the invention of gunpowder and the sailors' compass to paper and printing. Technologically, China was about 500 years ahead of Europe.

- **The Song period** is also known for its exquisite landscape paintings and fine porcelain, which is why good porcelain is called 'China'.

- **In 1126,** barbarian invasions forced the Song to move their capital from Kaifeng in the north to Hangzhou (modern Shanghai) in the south.

- **By 1275**, Hangzhou was the world's largest city, with a population of a million. Its warm climate encouraged a lively, leisurely lifestyle. The city was full of luxury shops, bars, restaurants, tea-houses and clubs where girls sang. Often, people went out to stroll in the gardens by the West Lake or lazed over long meals on the lake's scores of floating restaurants, pushed along by poles like Venetian gondolas. Marco Polo later complained that the people here were 'anything but warriors; all their delight was in women, nothing but women.'

FASCINATING FACT
The Song inventions gunpowder and printing had a huge influence on Europe when, they arrived there centuries later.

Joan of Arc

- **St Joan of Arc** (c.1412-31) was the peasant girl who led France from defeat in the Hundred Years' War and was burned at the stake for her beliefs.

- **Joan** was called Jeanne d'Arc in France. She called herself Jeanne la Pucelle (Joan the Maid).

- **Joan** was brought up in the village of Domrémy, near Nancy, northeastern France, as a shepherd girl.

- **By the age of 13,** Joan was having visions and believed that God had chosen her to help the French king Charles VII to beat the English.

- **Joan tried** to see the king but was laughed at until she was finally admitted to the king's court, in 1429.

▲ *Known traditionally as the Maid of Orléans, Joan was made a saint in 1920.*

- **To test Joan**, the king stood in disguise amongst his courtiers but Joan recognized him instantly – and also told him what he asked for in his secret prayers.

- **Joan was given** armour and an army to rescue the town of Orléans from the English and succeeded in just ten days.

- **Joan then** led Charles VII through enemy territory to be crowned at Rheims cathedral.

- **In May 1430,** Joan was captured by the English and accused of witchcraft.

- **Joan insisted that** her visions came from God, so a tribunal of French clergy condemned her as a heretic. She was burned at the stake in Rouen on 30 May 1431.

▼ *It was said that a short-haired, armour-clad Joan, flying her own flag, pushed back the English at Orléans, in 1429. She then took the Dauphin to Rheims, to be crowned Charles VII.*

Knights

- **Knights** were the elite fighting men of the Middle Ages, highly trained for combat both on horseback and on foot.

- **Knights always wore** armour. At first, the armour was simply shirts of mail, made from linked rings of iron. By the 1400s, most knights wore full suits of plate armour.

- **Knights rode into battle** on a horse called a destrier, or warhorse, and usually had an easy-going horse called a palfry just for travelling, plus a packhorse called a sumpter.

- **Knights had a strict** code of honour called chivalry – from *chevalier*, the French for 'horseman'.

▶ *Medieval knights were always ready to fight to defend their own honour and that of their lord.*

46

- **The ideal knight** was meant to be bold but good and gentle – fighting only to defend his lord, his lady and the Church. But in reality many were just brutal fighting men.

- **Training to be a knight** was a long and costly process, so most were from wealthy families.

- **A young boy** training to be a knight began at 7 as a page to a lord, then became a knight's squire (apprentice) at 14.

- **A squire's task** was to look after his master's armour, dress him for battle and serve his food.

- **A squire** who passed all the tests was dubbed a 'knight' at about 21 years old.

- **Knights took part** in mock battles called tournaments, often involving 'jousts', where two knights would charge at each other with lances.

▶ *This is a typical design of an 11th century shield. As knights wore more and more plate armour, their shields were made smaller.*

47

The Renaissance

▼ This portrayal of God's Creation of Man comes from the great Renaissance artist Michelangelo's famous paintings on the ceiling of the Sistine Chapel, in Rome.

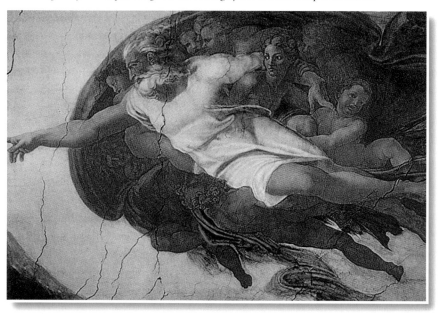

- **The Renaissance** was the great revolution in arts and ideas in Italy between the 1300s and the 1500s.

- **Renaissance** is French for 'rebirth', because it was partly about a revival of interest in the works of the classical world of Greece and Rome.

- **The Renaissance began** when many people started to doubt that the Church had all the answers.

- **Scholars** gradually developed the idea of 'humanism' – the idea that man is the focus of things, not God.

- **A spur** to the Renaissance was the fall of Constantinople in 1453. This sent Greek scholars fleeing to Italy, where they set up academies in cities like Florence and Padua.

- **Artists** in the Renaissance, inspired by classical examples, began to try and put people at the centre of their work – and to portray people and nature realistically rather than as religious symbols.

- **In the 1400s** brilliant artists like Donatello created startlingly realistic paintings and sculptures.

- **The three greatest artists** of the Renaissance were Michelangelo, Raphael and Leonardo da Vinci.

- **The Renaissance** saw some of the world's greatest artistic and architectural masterpieces being created in Italian cities such as Florence and Padua.

- **During the late 1400s,** Renaissance ideas spread to northern Europe.

▶ *Many Renaissance painters ran studios where a team of artists worked on a 'production line' principle, so that the painter himself was not wholly responsible for the work.*

The Mogul Empire

- **The Moguls,** or Mughals, were a family who ruled most of northern India from 1526 to 1748.

- **The Moguls** were descended from the Mongol Ghengis Khan via Tamerlane – the great conqueror of the 1300s.

- **The first Mogul** emperor was Babur (1483-1530), who invaded India on swift horses that completely outran the Indians' slower elephants.

- **Babur** was a brave and brilliant leader, as well as a famous poet and diarist.

- **Babur** created gardens wherever he went and held garden parties there when they were finished.

- **After Babur** came a string of remarkable emperors: Humayun, Akbar, Jahangir, Shah Jahan and Aurangzeb.

- **Akbar** (1556-1605) was the greatest of the Mogul emperors – conquering most of India and setting up a highly efficient system of government.

- **Jahangir** (1569-1627) was a great patron of the arts – but suffered from an addiction to drugs and alcohol. He was also attacked for being under the thumb of his Persian wife, Nur Jahan.

- **The Mogul Empire** reached its peak under Shah Jahan (1592-1666), when many magnificent, luxurious buildings were built – most notably the Taj Mahal.

- **Aurangzeb** (1618-1707) was the last great Mogul ruler. He inspired rebellion by raising taxes and insisting on a strict Muslim code.

▶ *Babur, or Zahir-ud-din Muhammad Babur in full, became the first Mogul emperor, occupying Agra and Delhi in 1526.*

▲ *The breathtaking Taj Mahal, at Agra in northern India, is perhaps the finest example of Mogul architecture. It was built by Mogul emperor Shah Jahan as a tomb for, and love-letter to, his favourite wife – Mumtaz Mahal.*

Voyages of exploration

- **In the late 1300s,** the Mongol Empire in Asia collapsed and Ottoman Turks grew powerful in the Near East. Roads to China and the east were cut off.

- **Italian merchant cities** like Genoa and Venice needed another route. So bold sailors set out from Portugal and Spain to find a way to the east by sea.

▼ *Nearly all European explorers sailed in caravels. These ships were rarely more than 20-30 m long and weighed under 150 tonnes. But they could cope with rough seas and head into the wind, so could sail in most directions. They were also fast – vital when crossing vast oceans.*

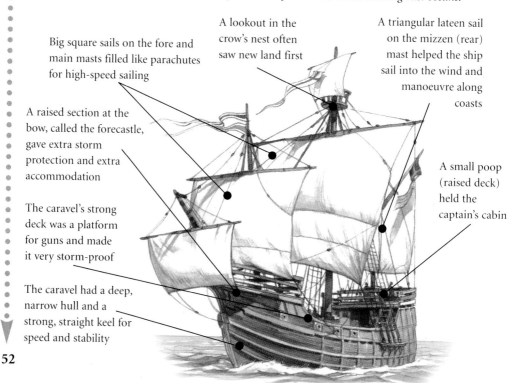

Big square sails on the fore and main masts filled like parachutes for high-speed sailing

A lookout in the crow's nest often saw new land first

A triangular lateen sail on the mizzen (rear) mast helped the ship sail into the wind and manoeuvre along coasts

A raised section at the bow, called the forecastle, gave extra storm protection and extra accommodation

A small poop (raised deck) held the captain's cabin

The caravel's strong deck was a platform for guns and made it very storm-proof

The caravel had a deep, narrow hull and a strong, straight keel for speed and stability

- **At first,** they tried to go round Africa, and voyages ventured down Africa's unknown west coast.

- **Many early voyages** were encouraged by Portugal's Prince Henry (1394-1460), who set up a school of navigation at Sagres.

- **In 1488,** Bartholomeu Dias sailed round Africa's southern tip and into the Indian Ocean.

- **In 1497,** Vasco da Gama sailed round Africa to Calicut in India, and returned laden with spices and jewels.

- **Perhaps the greatest** voyage by a European was in 1492, when Genoese sailor Christopher Columbus set out across the open Atlantic. He hoped to reach China by travelling westwards around the world. Instead, he found the whole 'New World' – North and South America.

- **Columbus** only landed on Caribbean islands at first. Even when he reached South America on his last voyage, he thought he was in Asia. The first to realize it was an unknown continent was the Florentine explorer Amerigo Vespucci, who landed there in 1499. A map made in 1507 named North and South America after him.

- **In 1519-22,** Magellan's ship *Victoria* sailed across the Atlantic, round the southern tip of South America, across the Pacific and back round Africa to Spain. Although this Portuguese explorer was killed in the Philippines, his crew and ship went on to complete the first round-the-world voyage.

> **FASCINATING FACT**
> Venetian John Cabot set out from Bristol, England in 1497 – and 'discovered' North America when he landed in Labrador.

The Medicis

- **The Medici family** of Florence in Italy were one of the richest and most powerful families in Europe between 1400 and 1700.

- **The Medicis' fortunes** began with the bank founded by Giovanni Medici in 1397. The bank was a success and the Medicis became staggeringly rich.

- **Giovanni's son,** Cosimo, built up the bank and there were soon branches in major cities in Europe.

- **By 1434,** Cosimo was so rich and powerful that he became ruler of Florence. Except for brief periods, the Medicis then ruled Florence for 300 years.

- **The Medicis** were famed for paying huge sums of money to commission works of art.

▲ *Lorenzo de' Medici was a tough ruler who put down opposition brutally. But he was also a scholar and a fine poet.*

- **The artist** Michelangelo worked for the Medicis from 1515 to 1534 and created the fabulous Medici chapel for them.

- **The most famous Medici** was Lorenzo (1449-92), known as the Magnificent. Under him, Florence became Europe's most splendid city, full of great works of art.

▲ *During the 1400s, art and architecture in Florence flourished under the Medicis' patronage. The city's magnificent domed cathedral was the work of Renaissance architect, Brunelleschi.*

- **Lorenzo** may have been Magnificent, but he managed to bankrupt the Medici bank.

- **Three Medicis** became pope – Leo X (1513-21), Clement VII (1523-34) and then Leo XI (1605).

- **Two Medicis** became queens of France. One of these was Catherine de' Medici (1519-89), queen of Henry II.

The Incas

- **The Incas** were South American people who created a remarkable empire in the Americas in the 1400s.

- **The Incas** began as a tribe in highland Peru, but in 1438 Pachacuti Inca Yupanqui became their Sapa Inca (king) and they built a huge empire in an amazingly short time.

- **Pachacuti** and his son built a huge empire in just 50 years stretching 4000 km through what is now Peru and Chile.

- **Inca soldiers** were highly disciplined and deadly with slings, bronze axes and spears.

- **Inca engineers** swiftly built 30,000 km of paved roads across the empire, spanning deep ravines with dizzying suspension bridges.

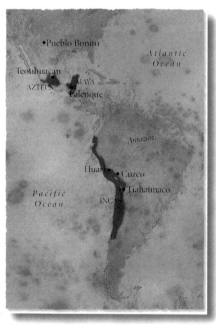

▲ *The darker brown area shows the extent of the Inca empire at the height of its power.*

- **The Incas** kept in close touch with local officials by relays of runners 2.5 km apart. A message could travel 250 km in under a day.

- **Inca builders** cut and fitted huge stones with astonishing precision to create massive buildings.

- **The royal palace** had a garden full of life-like corn stalks, animals and birds made of solid gold.

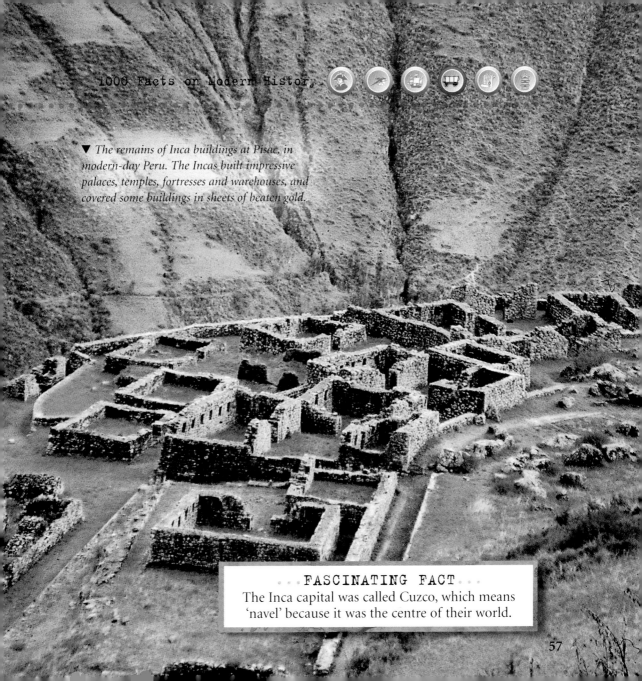

▼ *The remains of Inca buildings at Pisac, in modern-day Peru. The Incas built impressive palaces, temples, fortresses and warehouses, and covered some buildings in sheets of beaten gold.*

. . . FASCINATING FACT . . .
The Inca capital was called Cuzco, which means 'navel' because it was the centre of their world.

57

Christopher Columbus

▶ *The beautiful shores of the Bahamas were probably those first spotted by Columbus on his voyage westward.*

- **Christopher Columbus** (1451-1596) was the Genoese sailor who crossed the Atlantic and 'discovered' North and South America for Europe.

- **Columbus** was not the first European to cross the Atlantic. The Vikings, for instance, settled in Newfoundland in AD 1004. But it is Columbus's discovery that lasted.

- **Other sailors** were trying to find their way to China and the east by sailing south round Africa. Columbus, realizing the Earth is round, wanted to strike out west across the open Atlantic Ocean and reach China that way.

- **After years spent trying** to get backing Columbus finally got support from Queen Isabella of Spain.

- **Columbus set sail** on 3 August 1492 in three caravels – the *Santa Maria*, the *Niña* and the *Pinta*.

- **They sailed west** into the unknown for three weeks, by which time the sailors were ready to mutiny with fear.

- **On 12 October**, a look-out spotted the Bahamas. Columbus thought he was in the Indies (hence the 'West Indies'). He called the native peoples Indians.

- **Columbus** left 40 men on a large island that he called Hispaniola and went back to Spain a hero.

- **In 1493 and 1498,** he set off on two more trips with large fleets, as Viceroy of the Indies. He set up a colony on Hispaniola, but it was a disaster. Spaniards complained of his harsh rule and many Indians died from cruelty and disease. Columbus went back to Spain in chains.

- **Columbus** was pardoned, and began a fourth voyage in 1502. He died off Panama, still thinking it was India.

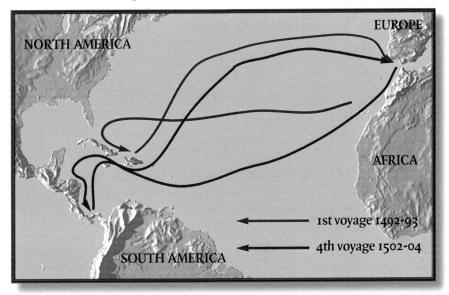

▲ *Columbus's first and last voyages*

The Reformation

● **In the early 1500s,** many people were starting to question the teachings of the Catholic Church. They were angered by the power of church leaders and the life of idleness that many monks seemed to lead.

▲ *St Peter's Basilica, Rome – the world's largest Christian church. Begun in 1506, this costly undertaking was partly funded by pardons 'sold' by the pope.*

● **Many critics were angered** by the amounts of money the Church made by selling 'indulgences' – a pardon for sin bought with cash.

● **Martin Luther** (1483-1546) was a poor miner's son from Saxony in Germany. As a monk at Wittenberg University, he earned a reputation for his great biblical knowledge.

● **Luther** attacked the sale of 'indulgences' (pardons for sin) by Pope Leo X, who was selling them by the score to raise money to build St Peter's church in Rome.

● **In 1517,** Luther nailed a list of 95 grievances on the door of Wittenberg Castle's chapel, hoping to start a debate.

- **The pope** issued a bull (demand) that Luther go back on his views or face expulsion from the Church. Luther burned the bull – and the Church expelled him in 1521.

- **The development of printing in Europe in the 1400s** meant that pamphlets explaining Luther's views could be read by thousands, and support grew rapidly.

- **Luther set up** his own church, whose members soon came to be called Protestants – because of their protests.

- **Other more extreme rebels** joined the cause, such as John Calvin (1509-64) and Ulrich Zwingli (1484-1531), and the movement gathered pace across northwest Europe.

- **Soon the Protestant** movement was so strong and widespread that the split with the Catholic Church seemed permanent. This is called the Reformation.

▶ *Martin Luther was the monk whose radical views sparked off the great Reformation, which divided Christians in Europe into Catholics and Protestants.*

The conquistadors

- **The conquistadors** ('conquerors') were Spaniards who landed in the 'New World' shortly after Columbus. They came to conquer the peoples there.

- **The most famous** conquistadors were Hernán Cortés (1485-1547) and Francisco Pizarro (c.1478-1541).

- **Cortés landed** in Mexico with just 500 men in 1519. The Indian girl Malintzin became his interpreter and lover.

- **Joining** with Indians rebelling against the Aztecs, he marched to Tenochtitlán, the Aztec capital (present-day Mexico City).

▼ *The Aztec people of Central America created a great, advanced civilization – until Cortés's conquistadors finally crushed it, in 1521.*

- **Perhaps thinking** that Cortés was the god Quetzalcoatl, the Aztec leader Moctezuma let Cortés take him prisoner and become ruler in his place.

- **When Cortés** left Tenochtitlán six months later, the Aztecs rebelled. Cortés returned and destroyed the city.

- **Pizarro** set off to find the Incas in 1524.

- **Pizarro** reached Peru when the Incas were hardly over a civil war between the Inca Atahualpa and his brother.

- **The Incas,** terrified of Pizarro's horses and guns, were easily slaughtered. Pizarro took Cuzco in 1533.

▶ *The typical conquistador was essentially an adventurer and bounty-hunter, ill-suited to the job of ruling. Once the conquistadors had defeated local peoples, Spanish administrators moved in to govern the region.*

···**FASCINATING FACT**···
When Spaniards got off their horses, the Incas thought they were beasts splitting in two.

Shoguns and samurai

- **In the 12th century,** the civilized Japanese Fujiwara rulers were replaced by powerful warrior clans from country areas – notably the Taira and Minamoto.

- **In 1185,** the Minamoto Yoritomo crushed the Taira clan and made himself ruler of Japan as sei-i-dai-shogun, which means 'barbarian conquering great general'.

- **Warrior shoguns** ruled Japan until the mid-1800s.

- **Japan** became dominated by samurai. The samurai warriors lived to fight and trained in fighting skills to a fanatical degree.

- **A samurai's prized possession** was his massive two-handed sword, which was sharpened and honed to such an extent that a skilled samurai could slice a man in half with a single stroke.

- **Samurai** means 'one who serves'.

▼ *Samurai warriors dominated Japan for centuries.*

- **The warrior culture** drove many to seek refuge in nature and men started to live for long periods in remote huts.

- **A kind of Buddhism** called Zen appealed to many Japanese. It showed how meditation could make them see beyond the material world.

- **In the 1300s** Samurai began to take a more Zen approach to their skills.

- **In the 1300s** these Zen Buddhists began to develop their own forms of elegant entertainment, like flower-arranging and tea-drinking.

▲ *Today it is fashionable all around the world to incorporate Zen principles in the home and garden. The simple lines of this Zen garden promote calm feelings of peaceful meditation.*

Henry VIII

- **Henry VIII** (1491-1547) was the Tudor king of England who separated the Church in England from Rome, and who married six wives, beheading two of them.

  - **Henry's wives:** Catherine of Aragon (1509-33, divorced); Anne Boleyn (1533-36, beheaded); Jane Seymour (1536-38, died); Anne of Cleves (1540, annulled); Catherine Howard (1540-42, beheaded); and Catherine Parr (1543-47).

  - **When Henry VIII** became king at 18, in 1509, he was handsome and athletic, spoke several languages, played the lute well and was keen on new 'humanist' ideas. As he grew old, he became grossly fat, riddled with sickness and inclined to terrible outbreaks of anger.

  - **Henry was served** by clever ministers like Wolsey and Cromwell. Many were executed when things went wrong.

◀ *We have an astonishingly clear picture of what Henry and his court looked like from the brilliant portraits of Hans Holbein. This picture is based on Holbein's striking painting of Henry from 1537.*

▶ *Catherine Parr – the only one of Henry VIII's six wives to survive him.*

- **Catherine of Aragon** bore Henry a daughter, Mary, but not the needed son. The pope refused a divorce, so Henry broke with Rome to become head of the English Church.

- **Split from Rome,** the Church of England moved towards Protestantism and the monasteries were destroyed.

- **Anne Boleyn** gave Henry a daughter, Elizabeth, but not the son he wanted, and her strong views made her enemies. She was beheaded on a charge of treason.

- **Jane Seymour** gave Henry a son, Edward, but died in childbirth in 1538.

- **Henry** found Anne of Cleves so ugly, he cancelled the marriage after five months.

- **Young Catherine Howard** was beheaded when she was found to have a lover. Only Henry's last wife, twice-widowed Catherine Parr, survived him when he died in 1547.

Catholics v Protestants

- **In the 1500s** the Roman Catholic Church was determined to fight against the Protestant Reformation and other threats. Their fight is called the Counter-Reformation.

- **In 1534,** St Ignatius Loyola founded the Society of Jesus (Jesuits) to lead the Counter-Reformation.

- **Investigative bodies** called Inquisitions were set up to seek out and punish heretics – anyone who held views that did not agree with the Catholic Church's.

- **From 1483,** the Spanish Inquisition became a byword for terror, swooping on suspected heretics – Protestants and Jews alike – torturing them and burning them at the stake.

▲ *Thomas More (1478-1535) was executed when he refused to acknowledge Henry VIII as head of the English Church.*

- **The battle between** Catholics and Protestants created many victims and many martyrs in the late 1500s.

- **In the St Bartholomew's Day massacre** in 1571, up to 70,000 French Protestants, called Huguenots, were killed on the orders of the Catholic queen Catherine de' Medici.

◄ *The Spanish Inquisition was notorious for public burnings of anyone they considered to be dangerously anti-Catholic. Their activities continued until the 1800s.*

- **English Protestants** were burned in Catholic Queen Mary's reign, earning her the name 'Bloody Mary'.

- **English Catholics** such as Edmund Campion (1540-1581) were hanged, drawn and quarteres in Protestant Queen Elizabeth I's reign.

- **In Germany,** a terrible Thirty Years' War was started in 1618 as Catholic-Protestant rivalries flared up.

> ...FASCINATING FACT...
> Catholic houses in England in the late 1500s
> had hiding places for priests called 'priest holes'.

The Spanish Empire

- **Within half a century** of Columbus's arrival in America in 1492, Spanish conquistadors had conquered Latin America – from California to Argentina.

- **By the Treaty of Tordesillas (1494)** Portugal allowed Spain to take any territory more than 370 leagues (about 2000 km) west of the Cape Verde islands – all of Latin America but Brazil.

- **Thousands of Spaniards** came to colonize Latin America in the 1500s, creating cities such as Cartagena in Colombia and Guayaqil in Ecuador.

Hull and decking of winter-cut oak, cedar or cypress hardwood

Three masts with square sails – or, as here, with a triangular lateen on the mizzen (rear) mast

Banks of 20 or so cannon for 'broadsides' – firing together down one side

◄ *Once a year, two Spanish treasure fleets would leave from Havana in Cuba guarded by the galleons of the Armada de la Guardia. Galleons were the biggest warships, 35 m long and weighing around 500 tonnes.*

- **The Spanish rulers** tried to deal with local people with the *encomienda*, whereby Native Americans were assigned to Spaniards who were supposed to look after them in return for taxes and labour. In practice, many Spaniards were cruel to these people, and Spaniards now talk of how cruelly they abused the Native Americans. In 100 years, the number of Native Americans dropped from 50 million to 4 million, through cruelty, poverty and diseases brought by Spaniards.

- **Many Spanish Dominican friars** condemned the *encomienda* – especially Bartolomé de Las Casas – and fought unsuccessfully for better conditions for Native Americans.

- **Indians mined** silver, gold and gems in huge amounts in South America. The Muzo and Chivor mines in Colombia were famous for their emeralds.

- **Every year**, in the calm months between March and October, ships laden with treasure left the Americas bound for Spain.

- **Besides American** treasure, Spanish ships carried spices from the East Indies and silks from China. These were shipped across the Pacific from the Philippines to Mexico, then carried overland to be shipped from the Caribbean to Europe.

- **By the 1540s,** the Spanish ships were suffering pirate attacks, so the ships crossed the Atlantic every year in two great *flotas* (fleets) protected by an armada of galleons (warships).

> ... **FASCINATING FACT** ...
> The Spanish brought new foods such as tomatoes, potatoes and chocolate back to Europe from their American empire.

Elizabeth I

● **Elizabeth I** (1533-1603) was one of England's greatest rulers. The time of her reign is called the Elizabethan Age or England's Golden Age. Under her strong and intelligent rule, England became an enterprising, artistically rich and peaceful nation.

● **Elizabeth** was daughter of Henry VIII and his wife Anne Boleyn, who was beheaded when Elizabeth was three.

● **Elizabeth** was a brilliant scholar, fluent in many languages by the time she was 12.

● **When Henry VIII died,** Elizabeth's nine-year-old half-brother became King Edward VI, but he died in 1553. He was succeeded by her older sister 'Bloody' Mary.

◀ *Elizabeth loved the theatre. Here, Shakespeare himself (at the front of the acting group) performs in a play in front of the queen.*

▶ *William Shakespeare was one of several important English writers whose work flourished during Elizabeth I's reign.*

- **Mary was** staunchly Catholic. For a while Elizabeth was locked up, suspected of involvement in a Protestant plot.

- **Elizabeth became queen** in 1558, when Mary died.

- **At once** Elizabeth strengthened the Protestant Church of England by the Act of Supremacy in 1559.

- **Elizabeth was expected** to marry, and she encouraged foreign suitors when it helped diplomacy. But she remained single, earning her the nickname 'The Virgin Queen'.

- **Elizabeth** sent troops to help Protestants in Holland against their Spanish rulers, and secretly urged Francis Drake to raid Spanish treasure ships. In 1588 Spain sent an Armada to invade England. Elizabeth proved an inspiring leader and the Armada was repulsed.

- **Elizabeth's reign** is famed for the poetry and plays of men like Spenser, Marlowe and Shakespeare.

The colonization of America

▲ *'Pilgrims' on their way to church. Pilgrims were devout Puritans who had been persecuted for their beliefs in England and so set up a colony in America in the 1600s.*

- **In the 1580s,** English people tried unsuccessfully to set up colonies in North America.

- **The first successful English colony** was set up at Jamestown, Virginia on 24 May 1607, with 104 colonists.

- **Many of the Jamestown colony** died in 'the starving time' of winter 1609.

- **In 1610,** fighting broke out with the local Indians as the desperate colonists took the Indians' food supply.

- **Colonist leader** John Smith was captured by the Indians, but the chief's daughter, Pocahontas, saved his life.

- **In 1612,** colonist John Rolfe introduced tobacco from the West Indies. It became the basis of Virginia's economy.

- **Pocahontas** was held hostage by the colonists in 1613. While captive she met, fell in love with and wed John Rolfe.

- **In December 1620,** 102 'Pilgrims' arrived from Plymouth, England in the *Mayflower* and set up a new colony near Cape Cod. They survived thanks to help from Wampanoag Indians.

- **In November 1621** the Pilgrims invited the Wampanoags to celebrate their first harvest. This first Thanksgiving Day is now celebrated every year in the USA.

▶ *Daughter of a Native American chief, Pocahontas wed prominent colonist John Rolfe.*

FASCINATING FACT
Pocahontas died of influenza while in London, raising money for the colonists.

Dutch independence

- **In 1500** there were 17 provinces making up what is now Belgium, the Netherlands and Luxembourg. The most important was Holland.

- **The provinces came** under Spanish rule in 1516, when their ruler Charles became the king of Spain.

- **In the 1500s,** Holland's capital Amsterdam became the leading commercial centre of Europe. With the growth of trade, Protestant ideas started taking hold.

- **Charles's son** Philip II and his deputy the duke of Alba tried to crush the Protestants by executing their leaders.

- **As Alba** became more ruthless, opposition spread.

- **In 1566,** William, prince of Orange, led the Dutch in revolt. Although the Dutch controlled the sea, they gradually gave way before the Spanish army.

- **In 1574,** the Dutch opened dikes holding back the sea to sail over the flood to Leiden and rescue the besieged.

- **Protestants** retreated to the northern provinces, and in 1581 declared themselves the independent Dutch Republic. The fighting ceased.

- **The 1600s** proved a Golden Age for the Dutch Republic.

- **The Dutch** merchant fleet became the biggest in Europe. Dutch banks and businesses thrived and Dutch scientists like Leeuwenhoek and Huygens made great discoveries.

▶ *In the 1400-1600s, Dutch artists like Steen, Vermeer and Rembrandt created vibrant, technically brilliant paintings, often of everyday scenes. This is by Van Eyck, who was said to have invented oil painting in the 1430s.*

Toyotomi Hideyoshi

- **Toyotomi Hideyoshi** (1536-81) was the great Japanese shogun who unified Japan.

- **Hideyoshi** was the son of poor, hard-working peasants.

- **As a boy,** Hideyoshi believed that if he became a shogun, he'd make sure peasants wouldn't have to work so hard.

- **As a man,** Hideyoshi became a soldier for shogun Oda Nobunaga, who was trying to unify Japan through force.

- **One day,** legend says, Hideyoshi warmed Nobunaga's shoes for a winter walk. Nobunaga made him a general.

▲ *Hideyoshi helped to perfect the Japanese art of making and taking tea.*

- **Hideyoshi** proved himself a brilliant general, and when Nobunaga was murdered, Hideyoshi carried on his work in unifying Japan – but by good rule as well as by arms.

- **By 1591**, Hideyoshi had unified Japan, but he kept warriors and peasants firmly separated as classes.

- **To establish** a mystique for his court, Hideyoshi had the Zen master Sen No Rikkyu perfect the tea ceremony.

- **Later, Hideyoshi** became paranoid. Suspecting his chief adviser Hidetsugu of plotting, he had Hidetsugu's family killed – including the beautiful Princess Komahime.

- **Komahime's father** Yoshiaki sided decisively with Hideyoshi's enemy, the hero Tokugawa Ieyasu, in the great battle that led to Hideyoshi's downfall.

▲ *Hideyoshi did much to develop international trade, and in 1597 became the first person to ban the Christian religion on political grounds.*

Russia

- **In 1237,** Tatar hordes, the descendants of Genghis Khan, swept into Russia, burning cities and slaughtering people. The Tatars stayed there for 200 years.

- **Some Russians** thrived under the Tatars and a trading post called Moscow grew into a powerful city at the centre of a province called Muscovy. In 1318, Prince Yuri of Moscow married the Tatar Khan's sister. A later prince called Ivan began collecting taxes for the Tatars.

- **Moscow** grew strong as the Tatars grew weak. In 1453, Ivan III ('the Great'), Grand Prince of Muscovy, was strong enough to drive out the Tatars.

- **Russians were Christians** of the Eastern Church ruled from Constantinople. Constantinople had become the second focus of Christianity when Rome fell to barbarians in the AD 400s. When Constantinople fell to the Turks in 1453, Ivan III called for Moscow to be the Third Rome. He wed a Byzantine princess, and his grandson Ivan IV took the title czar after the Roman caesars.

- **Ivan's** ambitions left him in need of money and food, so he forced thousands of peasants into serfdom – at a time when peasants in western Europe were gaining their freedom. Those who would not submit fled to the southern steppes, where they became known as Cossacks.

▶ *Ivan rebuilt Moscow's Kremlin as a vast, walled complex of palaces and churches. It has remained the centre of Russian government ever since.*

- **Ivan IV** (1544-84), the first czar, drove the Tatars out of Russia altogether, conquering Kazan, Astrakhan and much of Siberia – creating the first Russian Empire.

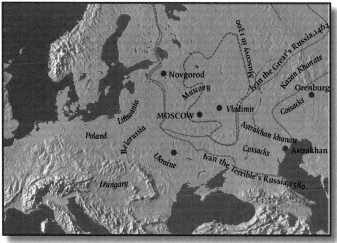

▲ *Under Ivan the Great and his grandson Ivan the Terrible, Russia grew to be a great empire.*

- **Ivan IV** was called 'the Terrible' for his brutality. He formed the Oprichniki – a police force to control people – and had hundreds of boyars (aristocrats) murdered. He even beat his son Ivan to death in a fit of rage.

- **Ivan IV** was an effective ruler, who encouraged scholars and brought Moscow its first printing presses.

- **Ivan IV's second son** Fyodor was a simpleton, and his wife's brother Boris Godunov seized the throne in 1598.

- **When Godunov died** in 1606, Moscow fell into a period of chaos called the 'Time of Troubles'. A monk called Gregory Otrepiev claimed to be Dmitry, another of Ivan IV's sons who was thought to have died. He invaded Moscow with a Polish army and rebellious Cossacks, and Russia was torn apart by civil war.

Mary Queen of Scots

- **Mary Queen of Scots** (1542-87) was the Catholic queen of Scotland held captive in England by Elizabeth I for 19 years, then beheaded.

- **Mary became queen** when she was a baby but was brought up at the French court, where she enjoyed hunting and learned six languages.

- **Mary married** the French king Henry II's son Francis at 15 and was briefly queen of France, but Francis died in 1560.

- **In 1561,** Mary returned to Scotland to rule there. By this time, Scotland had become Protestant, while Mary was a Catholic.

- **In 1565,** Mary fell in love with her cousin Henry Stuart, Earl of Darnley. She married him and they had a child, but Darnley was only interested in power.

- **Led by Darnley,** Protestant nobles stabbed Mary's Catholic secretary David Rizzio to death before her.

- **The Earl of Bothwell** was in love with Mary and murdered Darnley. They married three months later. The Scots were so outraged by the marriage that Mary had to flee to England.

◀ *Mary with her cousin and second husband, the highly ambitious Earl of Darnley – an ill-starred marriage that ended in deception and double murder.*

82

- **Mary** was next in line to the English throne after Elizabeth. Many Catholics felt she was first in line, since they did not recognize Henry VIII's marriage to Anne Boleyn.

- **Mary** posed a danger to Elizabeth, so she was kept in captivity in English houses, where she became the focus for plots against Elizabeth.

- **Elizabeth's spy-master** Walsingham trapped Mary into going along with a plot by Babington. Mary was found guilty of treason and beheaded at Fotheringay in 1587.

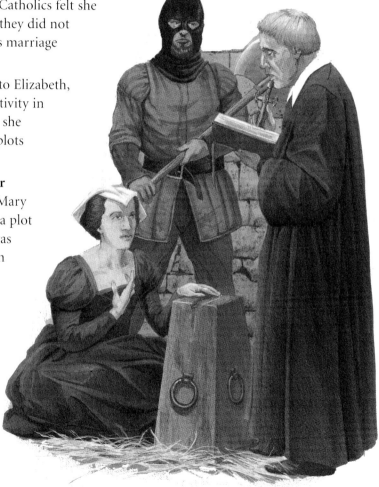

▶ *Mary about to meet her death at the executioner's block. Her presence in England had made her a dangerous focus for Catholic plots against Elizabeth I.*

Native Americans

- **When the first European colonists** arrived in North America, there were one and a half million Native Americans living in North America.

- **There were hundreds** of tribes in North America, each with its own language.

- **There were six** kinds of tribal area: the Southwest, Great Plains, Far West Plateau, Northwest, Eastern Woodland and Northern.

- **Southwest** Native Americans like the Pueblo Indians lived by growing corn, beans and squash.

- **Plains** tribes like the Blackfoot, Comanche and Cheyenne hunted buffalo on foot.

- **With Woodland tribes** like the Delaware, the men hunted deer and fished while the women grew crops.

- **Plateau and Northwest** Native Americans like the Nez Percé and the Kwakiutl lived by fishing and gathering berries. They are famous for their baskets.

- **Northern** tribes like the Cree lived mainly byhunting caribou.

- **Until Europeans** arrived, Native Americans got around mainly on foot or by canoe. The Europeans introduced horses in the 1700s – and Indians quickly became skilled riders.

◀ *Native North Americans typically wore 'buckskin' clothes – made from the tanned hides of deer. Eagle feathers provided decoration and held a special meaning.*

▲ *Native Indians who lived on the
Plains were often on the move,
looking for buffalo to hunt. As they
went from camp to camp they made
tepees, large tents built with poles
and covered by buffalo skins.*

... FASCINATING FACT ...
Woodland tribes lived in wigwams, domes
of sticks covered in hide and moss.

85

The Manchus

- **In the 1600s,** the Ming emperors of China were unpopular after three centuries in power. Rebellions became all too common.

- **In 1644,** the last Ming emperor hanged himself as the bandit Li Zicheng and his men overran Beijing.

- **Guarding the Great Wall** were Manchu troops, from Manchuria in the north. A desperate Ming general invited them to help get rid of Li Zicheng.

- **The Manchus** marched into Beijing and proclaimed their own child-emperor as the 'Son of Heaven' and set up the Qing dynasty of emperors.

- **Resistance** to the Manchu emperors went on in the south for 30 years, but was eventually suppressed.

- **At first, the Qing** forced Chinese men to put their hair in pigtails to show they were inferior to Manchus.

- **Manchus** and Chinese were also made to live separately and were not allowed to marry each other.

- **In time**, the Qing adopted Chinese ways, and even Manchu civil servants had to learn the classic works of Confucius, just like the Chinese.

- **Under the Qing,** China reached its greatest extent.

- **In the 1800s,** Qing power was weakened by rebellions, Muslim uprisings and growing European influence.

▲ *Under the Qing, China remained as it had been for 3000 years, while much of the world was changing dramatically.*

▲ *Manchu troops guarded China's ancient Great Wall against bandits, but the Manchus eventually seized power for themselves.*

Roundheads and Cavaliers

- **The English Civil War** (1642-49) was the struggle between 'Cavalier' supporters of King Charles I and 'Roundheads', who supported Parliament.

- **A key issue** was how much power the king should have. Charles wanted to be free to set taxes and his own brand of religion. Parliament demanded a say.

- **On the royalist side** were those, who wanted the English Church more Catholic; on the other were Puritans.

- **Puritans** were extreme Protestants. They believed that churches (and people) should be stripped of the wasteful luxury they saw in the Catholic Church and the aristocrats at the court of Charles's French, Catholic wife.

- **'Cavalier'** is from the French *chevalier* (horseman). It was meant as a term of abuse. Many Cavaliers were rich landowners.

- **Puritans** thought long hair indulgent, and the Roundheads got their name from their short-cropped hair. Many Roundheads were rich merchants and townspeople.

▶ *A Cavalier soldier. The term Cavalier was coined because many of Charles's supporters were seen as frivolous courtiers who loved fighting for its own sake.*

- **Many revolutionary groups** emerged among poorer people, such as the 'Diggers' and 'Levellers'.

- **The war** turned against the royalists when the parliamentarians formed the disciplined New Model Army.

- **Charles I** was beheaded in 1649.

- **Oliver Cromwell** (1599-1658) became Roundhead leader and signed Charles I's death warrant. In 1653, he made himself Lord Protector – England's dictator.

▶ *Many Cavaliers had long hair and wore colourful and elaborate clothes, after the style of the French court. Some, like Lovelace, were poets.*

The Sun King

- **Louis XIV** (1638-1715) was king of France for 72 years, a longer reign than any other European king in history.

- **Louis** became king in 1643, when he was five, and the first minister Cardinal Mazarin effectively ruled France.

- **In 1648,** heavy taxes and other grievances inspired a rebellion – the Fronde – against the hated Mazarin.

- **During the Fronde,** Louis was forced into hiding, and vowed never to let the same happen again.

- **Louis** said '*L'état c'est moi*' ('I am the State') and believed it was his God-given right to command his people totally.

- **When Mazarin died,** in 1661, Louis decided to run the country himself, and devoted huge energy to administering every detail of the nation's business.

- **Louis** made France the most efficiently run country in Europe. It hummed with new industries, road and canals.

- **Louis** used the finest artists to turn the French court into a glittering spectacle to distract nobles from rebellion. His palace was filled with banquets, plays and art.

- **Louis** got the nickname 'The Sun King' from his favourite dance role, that of Apollo the Sun God. He adopted the Sun as his emblem.

◀ *Louis used the image of the Sun in his emblem, as he loved to play the part of Apollo the Sun God in dances and masques.*

▲ *Court life at the magnificent palace and gardens of Versailles, just outside Paris, formed the stunning centrepiece of the Sun King's reign.*

FASCINATING FACT
Louis' magnificent new palace at Versailles took 36,000 workers 47 years to build.

Gustavus Adolphus

- **Gustavus Adolphus** (1594-1632) was Sweden's greatest king and military leader.

- **Gustavus** was a brilliant speaker and inspiring general who always led his men into battle from the front.

- **Gustavus** had a perfect ally in his chancellor Axel Oxenstierna (said 'erks'n'sherna'). Gustavus ran the foreign wars while Oxenstierna ran Sweden.

- **When Gustavus came** to the throne at the age of 17, Sweden was involved in three wars: with Denmark (1611-13), Russia (1611-17) and Poland.

- **Gustavus** quickly made peace with Denmark and Russia.

- **In skirmishes** with the Poles, Gustavus began to develop the first modern army – a large, highly mobile force combining foot soldiers and horsemen.

- **Gustavus** was a devout Protestant. When he saw the Protestants of Germany facing defeat in the Thirty Years' War against the Catholic Austrian emperor Ferdinand II, he decided to intervene.

- **In July 1630,** Gustavus's armies landed in Germany.

- **In 1631,** Gustavus won a great victory over Ferdinand's army at Breitenfeld near Leipzig.

- **On 6 Nov 1632,** the Swedes scored a crucial victory over Bohemian general Wallenstein, but Gustavus himself was killed leading a charge.

▶ *Gustavus's great flagship, the* Vasa, *sank on its maiden voyage in 1628, but it has been recovered almost intact and can now be seen in Stockholm.*

Pirates

▲ *The famous 'Jolly Roger' flag, flown from pirate ships.*

- **Barbary corsairs** were pirates from North Africa who raided ships in the Mediterranean between 1520 and 1830. Many corsairs were Muslims and regarded Christian merchant ships as fair game.

- **The most famous** corsairs were the Barbarossa brothers and Occhiali.

- **Sea dogs** were pirates like Sir Francis Drake, secretly encouraged by Queen Elizabeth I to raid the ships of her Spanish enemies in the Caribbean.

- **'Letters of marque'** from the monarch gave English raiders official blessing, so they were called privateers.

- **When King James I** withdrew letters of marque in 1603, privateers were replaced by lawless 'buccaneers' like Henry Morgan, who terrorized the Caribbean from bases on Jamaica like Port Royal.

- **Buccaneer** comes from the French *boucan* (barbeque) as many were poor hunters who grilled the meat of cows and pigs that they scavenged.

- **Piracy** reached its height between 1690 and 1790, preying on traders plying between Europe and its new colonies around the world.

- **In the Indian Ocean** were pirates like William Kidd from Madagascar. In the Bahamas, there was 'Calico Jack' Rackham and female pirates Anne Bonny and Mary Read.

- **The most notorious** pirate of this time was 'Blackbeard' (Edward Teach), who leaped into action with lighted firecrackers tied to his big black beard.

- **Piracy** diminished after 1720, when the British navy clamped down worldwide.

▼ *Female pirates Anne Bonny and Mary Read plied the high seas when piracy was at its height.*

The Restoration

- **For 11 years** after the execution of Charles I in 1649, England was without a king. It was ruled instead by the Commonwealth, run by the Puritans.

- **At first,** the Commonwealth consisted of Parliament and its Council of State, but its failure to make progress spurred general Oliver Cromwell to make himself Lord Protector and rule through army officers.

- **Cromwell's Protectorate** proved unpopular. When he died in 1658, the army removed his son Richard Cromwell as successor and called for Charles I's exiled son Charles II to be recalled as king.

- **The Restoration** of Charles II as king was in May 1660.

- **Charles II** proved on the whole a skilful ruler, tactfully easing tensions between rival religious groups.

- **Charles II** was known as the Merry Monarch, because his love of partying, theatre, horse-racing and women was such a relief after years of grim Puritan rule.

▶ *The sedan chair was a popular way for the rich to get about in the years after the Restoration.*

96

- **Charles II** had many mistresses. The most famous was Nell Gwyn, an orange-seller who worked in the theatre.

- **The Restoration** saw the Puritan ban on Christmas and the theatre lifted. Plays like Congreve's *Way of the World* made Restoration theatre lively and outrageous.

- **Charles II** took a keen interest in science, encouraging great scientists like Isaac Newton, Edmund Halley and Robert Hooke to form the Royal Society.

▲ *Exiled after his father's death, Charles first attempted to bring back the monarchy in 1651 but was defeated. After nine more years in exile, he was finally invited to return as king.*

FASCINATING FACT
When London burned down, in 1666, Charles II personally organized the fire-fighting.

Slavery

- **Slaves** were used a great deal in the ancient world, as warring people put their captives to work. The pyramids of Egypt were probably built mostly by slaves. One in three people in Ancient Athens was likely to have been a slave.

- **Slavery** diminished in Europe when Rome collapsed, although in the Middle Ages Russian and African slaves were used on sugar plantations in the Mediterranean.

- **Slavery** grew hugely when Europeans established colonies in the Americas from the 1500s on.

- **At first,** the settlers used Native Americans as slaves, but as numbers dwindled, they took slaves from Africa to work on new sugar plantations. British and French sugar planters in the West Indies used African slaves too.

▼ *Europeans established huge, highly profitable sugar plantations in the Caribbean, worked by African slaves who were treated appallingly.*

- **From 1500 to 1800,** Europeans shipped 10-12 million black slaves from Africa to the Americas. 40% went to Brazil, 30% to Cuba, Jamaica and Haiti, and 5% to the USA.

- **The slave trade** involved shipping several hundred thousand Africans across the Atlantic from the 'Slave Coast' of West Africa to the West Indies and the USA, or from Angola to Brazil. Once the slave ships had unloaded their slaves, they would return to Europe with a cargo of sugar, then sail for Africa with cotton goods and guns to exchange for slaves.

- **Slavery was rife** in the American south in the 1700s, where owners of large plantations needed cheap labour to grow first tobacco and then cotton.

- **In the West Indies** and Brazil, there were more blacks than whites and slaves often revolted. The greatest revolution was on French Haiti, where the slave Toussaint l'Ouverture (1743-1803) led 500,000 slaves to take over the country in 1791. For a while Haiti was black-governed – but Napoleon's troops reasserted control in 1802.

- **In the 1790s,** some Europeans began to speak out against slavery. Denmark banned the Atlantic slave trade in 1792. William Wilberforce got Britain to ban the trade in 1807. The USA banned the import of slaves in 1808. When Latin-American countries became independent in the early 1800s, they freed slaves. Britain abolished slavery in its empire in 1833, but the USA had to go through a civil war first.

FASCINATING FACT
Conditions on the slave ships were so dreadful that 2 million slaves died on them.

The Glorious Revolution

- **The Glorious Revolution** of 1688 was when the English Parliament replaced James II with William III and Mary, as king and queen.

- **James II** became king when his brother Charles II died in 1685.

- **James II** upset people by giving Catholics key jobs in the army, the Church and the universities.

- **James II** jailed any bishops who refused to support his Declaration of Indulgence in favour of Catholics.

- **In 1688,** James II and his Catholic wife Mary had a son. It seemed England was set to become Catholic.

- **Leading Protestants** decided to invite the Dutch prince William of Orange to help. William was married to James II's Protestant daughter Mary.

◀ *Mary sided with her Protestant husband, William, against her Catholic father James II.*

- **William landed** with his army at Brixham in Devon on 5 November 1688. James's army refused to obey its Catholic generals and so he was forced to flee to France.

- **Parliament** decided James's escape meant he had abdicated, and offered the throne to William and Mary.

- **James** tried a comeback, landing in Ireland with French troops. Defeat came at the Battle of the Boyne (July 1689).

▶ *William III, or William of Orange (1650-1702), suffered much political opposition and countless assassination plots in the latter years of his reign.*

. . . **FASCINATING FACT** . . .
Ulster Protestants are called Orangemen because
they once helped William of Orange at the Boyne.

The Age of Reason

- **The Age of Reason** is the time in the 1700s when many people began to believe that all-important questions about the world could be answered by reason.

- **The Age of Reason** is also called the Enlightenment.

- **The idea that human reason** has the answers was revolutionary. It meant that even the lowliest peasant was just as likely to be right as the highest lord. So why should a lord rule over a peasant?

- **In earlier times,** kings had ruled by 'divine right' – and their power over other people was God's will. The Age of Reason questioned this right.

- **As the 1700s** progressed, the ideas of the Age of Reason turned into real revolutions in France and America.

▶ *The French philosopher Diderot (1713-1784) spent much of his life compiling and writing the* Encyclopedia, *a work of reference that greatly reflected his views on philosophy and science.*

▶ Thomas Jefferson, *painted by John Trumbull.*
Jefferson (1743-1826) was America's third
president. He caught the spirit of the
age when he drafted the USA's
Declaration of Independence.

- **The hero of the Age**
  was Isaac Newton.
  His discovery of the
  Laws of Motion
  proposed that
  every single event
  in the Universe
  could be worked out
  mathematically.

- **American revolutionary**
  leader Jefferson had a
  portrait of Newton before him
  as he wrote the Constitution.

- **In France,** the great ideas were worked out by philosophers like Rousseau
  and Voltaire. People discussed the ideas earnestly at fashionable 'salons'
  (supper parties).

- **In Britain,** thinkers like Hume showed how important it was to work things
  out for yourself – not just be told.

- **To sum up all** human knowledge, the first great encyclopedia was created –
  by Diderot in France.

103

Peter the Great

- **Peter the Great** (1672-1725) was the greatest of all the Russian tsars (emperors). He built the city of St Petersburg and turned Russia from an inward-looking country to a major European power.

- **Peter was** well over 2 m tall, and towered above everyone else.

- **Peter had incredible** willpower and a burning interest in new ideas. But he was very impatient and often went into rages. When his son Alexei plotted against him, Peter had him put to death.

- **Peter became** tsar at the age of ten. His step-sister Sophia ruled for him until 1689, when her enemies drove her out and Peter took charge.

- **In 1697-98** Peter travelled to Holland and England disguised as a ship's carpenter in order to learn about western European technology and culture.

- **When Peter returned** from Europe, he brought with him many western European craftsmen and teachers.

- **Peter** insisted on Russian men shaving off their old-fashioned, Russian-style beards.

- **Peter** was very keen on boats. He built the first Russian navy – on the Volga River. His wars later ensured that Russia had, for the first time, a sea port on the Baltic.

- **Peter** led the Russian armies to crucial victories in battle – notably against the Swedes at Poltava in 1709.

- **Peter** created the first Russian Academy of Sciences, started Russia's first newspaper, and founded many schools, technical institutions and art galleries.

◄ *Legendary Russian tsar Peter the Great was a towering 2 m tall. He brought sweeping changes to Russia and carried many of them out with great brutality.*

▶ *The Cathedral of St Peter and St Paul, in St Petersburg – the grand city built by Peter the Great.*

British India

- **Shortly after** Vasco da Gama reached India, in 1498, the Portuguese set up a trading base in Goa.

- **In 1600,** Elizabeth I of England gave a charter to the East India Co. to trade in India. It set up posts at Surat, Madras, Bombay and Calcutta.

- **The French** set up a base at Pondicherry, in 1668.

- **In the 1700s,** rebellions weakened the Mogul empire. The French and British vied to gain control.

- **In 1757,** 3000 British soldiers, led by the East India Co.'s Robert Clive, defeated an army of over 50,000 French and Indian troops at the battle of Plassey.

- **After Clive's victory,** the British gradually gained control over much of India through a combination of bribes, bullying and making well-placed allies.

- **In 1803,** the British captured the Mogul capital of Delhi – so completing their power base.

- **British rule** was resented by many Indians. Hindus felt that the British were undermining their religion.

- **In 1857,** Indian soldiers revolted and other Indians joined them, but the 'mutiny' was crushed after 14 months.

- **In 1858,** the British decided to rule India directly. Their rule was called the Raj (which means 'rule'). In 1876, Queen Victoria of Britain was named empress of India.

▼ *Robert Clive's victory over Indian and French troops at the Battle of Plassey gave Britain control over much of India – control that would last for 200 years.*

American independence

- **In 1763,** Britain finally defeated the French in North America, adding Canada to its 13 colonies – but wanted the colonists to help pay for the cost. The colonists resented paying taxes to a government 5000 km away.

- **To avoid** costly wars with Native Americans, George III issued a Proclamation in 1763 reserving lands west of the Appalachians for native peoples and sent troops to keep settlers out, arousing colonists' resentment.

- **In 1764-5,** British prime minister Grenville brought in three new taxes – the Sugar Tax on molasses, which affected rum producers in the colonies; the Quartering Tax, which obliged the colonists to supply British soldiers with living quarters; and the Stamp Tax on newspapers, playing cards and legal documents.

- **Colonists** tolerated sugar and quartering taxes, but the Stamp Tax provoked riots. Delegates from nine colonies met in New York to demand a say in how they were taxed, demanding 'No taxation without representation.'

- **As protests** escalated, Grenville was forced to withdraw all taxes but one, the tax on tea. Then, in 1773, a crowd of colonists disguised as Mohawk Indians marched on to the merchant ship *Dartmouth* in Boston harbour and threw its cargo of tea into the sea. After this 'Boston Tea Party', the British closed Boston and moved troops in.

- **A Congress** of delegates from all the colonies except Georgia met to demand independence, and appointed George Washington to lead an army to fight their cause.

- **In April 1775,** British troops seized military stores at Lexington and Concord near Boston and the war began.

- **At first** the British were successful, but the problems of fighting 5000 km from home told in the long run. In 1781, Washington defeated the British at Yorktown, Virginia and they surrendered.

- **In 1776,** the colonists drew up a Declaration of Independence, written by Thomas Jefferson. The British recognized independence in 1783, and in 1787 the colonists drew up a Constitution to lay down how their Union should be run. In 1789, George Washington was elected as the first president of the United States of America.

◀ *The original 13 colonies of North America stretched from foggy Massachusetts in the north, 2500 km south to steamy Georgia. These 13 colonies became the first 13 states of the United States of America. The dates on the map show when they were founded. The green lines show today's states – these, of course, did not exist in 1775. In 1775, there were over 2.5 million people living in the colonies, with 450,000 in Virginia alone.*

(Map labels: Hudson Bay Company; Maine (part of Massachusetts); New Hampshire 1680; Massachusetts 1629; New York 1664; Rhode Island 1635; Connecticut 1664; New Jersey 1664; Pennsylvania 1681; Delaware 1702; Indian Reserve; 1763 Proclamation Line; Maryland 1632; Virginia 1607; N Carolina 1670; S Carolina 1670; Georgia 1732; West Florida; East Florida)

FASCINATING FACT
The Declaration of Independence began with the now famous words: 'We hold these truths to be self-evident, that all men are created equal, that they are endowed by their Creator with certain inalienable rights, and that among these are Life, Liberty and the pursuit of Happiness.'

The French Revolution

- **In 1789,** French people were divided among three 'Estates' – the nobles, clergy and middle class – plus the peasants. Nobles owned all the land, but were exempt from paying taxes, and the tax burden fell on the peasants.

- **In 1789,** France was bankrupt after many wars, and King Louis XVI was forced to summon Parliament, called the Estates General, for the first time in 175 years.

- **The three Estates** had met separately in the past, but now insisted on meeting in a National Assembly to debate how to limit the power of the king. The Assembly was dominated by the Third Estate, the middle class.

- **On 14 July 1789,** the poor people of Paris, tired of debates, stormed the prison fortress of the Bastille.

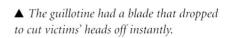

▲ *The guillotine had a blade that dropped to cut victims' heads off instantly.*

- **Fired by the fall** of the Bastille, peasants rose all over the country and refused to pay taxes. Parisian women marched to Versailles and dragged the king back to Paris.

- **The National Assembly** became more radical, ending serfdom and attacking the nobles and the Church. Many nobles fled the country in panic.

- **The Assembly** speakers who had the power to move the Paris mobs, like Georges Danton, came to the fore. The Assembly renamed itself the National Convention and set up the Committee of Public Safety to govern France by terror.

- **Many nobles** were sent to the guillotine and in 1793 Louis XVI and his queen, Marie Antoinette, were themselves guillotined.

- **This Reign of Terror** was presided over by Robespierre, who saw more and more of his rivals to the guillotine, including Danton. But in the end even Robespierre himself was guillotined, in July 1794.

- **With Robespierre gone,** conservatives regained control. Emphasis shifted to defending the revolution against foreign kings and to Napoleon's conquests.

▶ *When the French Revolution brought down the old ruling classes, crowds of ordinary people took to the streets to celebrate.*

Agricultural Revolution

- **The Agricultural Revolution** refers to dramatic changes in farming in Britain in the 1700s and later in the USA.

- **Before the 1700s,** farmland was mostly wide open fields, cultivated in narrow strips by peasants growing food for themselves, using traditional methods.

- **The Agricultural Revolution** created large farms, growing food for profit in enclosed fields, using specialist techniques.

- **The most dramatic effect** was enclosure, in which peasants were evicted from open fields as they were parcelled up into small fields for rearing livestock.

- **Crop-growing** was improved by techniques such as the four-field rotation system.

- **The four-field system** of 'Turnip' Townshend and Thomas Coke meant growing turnips, clover, barley and wheat in successive years so land was used all the time.

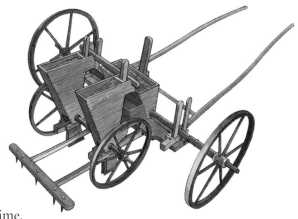

▲ *The first-ever seed drill was invented by Englishman Jethro Tull in 1701.*

- **Livestock farmers** found how to breed cattle, horses and sheep larger and fatter, like Bakewell's Leicester sheep.

- **New machines** were invented. Jethro Tull's drill, for example, made holes and planted seeds in them.

- **In 1793,** Eli Whitney invented a gin machine to separate cotton fibre from the seeds – so making large-scale cotton production profitable.

- **In 1834,** American Cyrus McCormick made the first mechanical harvester.

▲ *Separating the seeds from the fibres of cotton plants by hand is a very slow process. Once American farmer's son Eli Whitney invented the 'gin', mass-production became possible.*

Industrial Revolution

- **The Industrial Revolution** refers to the dramatic growth in factories that began in the 1700s.

- **Before the Industrial Revolution**, most ordinary people were farmers living in small villages. Afterwards, most were factory hands and foremen living in huge cities.

- **The Revolution** began in Britain in the late 1700s; in France, the USA and Germany in the early 1800s.

- **The Farming Revolution** created a pool of cheap labour, while the growth of European colonies created vast markets for things like clothing.

- **The Revolution** began with the invention of machines for making cloth, like the spinning jenny.

- **The turning point** was the change from hand-turned machines like the jenny to machines driven by big water wheels – like Arkwright's 'water powered spinning frame' of 1766.

- **In 1771,** Arkwright installed water frames at Crompton Mill, Derby and created the world's first big factory.

◄ *In 1764, Lancashire weaver James Hargreaves created the 'spinning jenny' to help cottage weavers spin wool or cotton fibres into yarn (thread) on lots of spindles, turned by a single handle.*

● **In the 1780s,** James Watt developed a steam engine to drive machines – and steam engines quickly replaced water as the main source of power in factories.

● **In 1713,** Abraham Darby found how to use coke, rather than wood charcoal, to make huge amounts of iron.

● **In 1784,** Henry Cort found how to remove impurities from cast iron to make wrought iron – and iron became the key material of the Industrial Revolution.

▶ *Arkwright's water frame, powered by a water wheel, used four pairs of rotating rollers to stretch fibres before they were spun.*

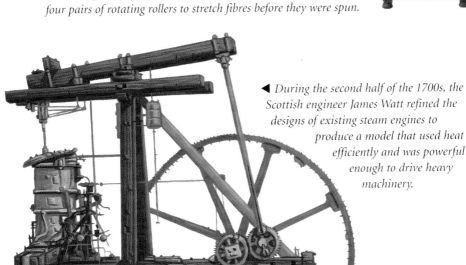

◀ *During the second half of the 1700s, the Scottish engineer James Watt refined the designs of existing steam engines to produce a model that used heat efficiently and was powerful enough to drive heavy machinery.*

The Jacobites

- **After James II** was deposed as king of England and Scotland in 1688, many Scots still believed he and his Stuart descendants were rightful kings.

- **Supporters** of the Stuarts were called Jacobites after *Jacobus*, Latin for James.

- **James II's** son James was called the Old Pretender, because he pretended to (claimed) the English throne.

- **English Queen Anne** died childless in 1714, and the Scottish and English Jacobites rose in revolt in 1715. This revolution is called 'the Fifteen'.

- **The Old Pretender** arrived in Scotland only after the Fifteen and its leaders had been crushed.

- **The Scots hero** of the Fifteen was Rob Roy MacGregor (1671-1734), an outlaw who stole cattle from English-inclined Duke of Montrose, then joined the rebellion. His tale is told in Walter Scott's novel *Rob Roy* (1817).

- **The Old Pretender's** son Charles was Bonnie Prince Charlie, the Young Pretender.

- **In 1745,** Bonnie Prince Charlie led the Jacobites in a rebellion – called 'the Forty-Five' – against George II.

◀ *Rob Roy MacGregor – Scottish outlaw, hero of the Jacobite rebellion of 1715 and the subject of Walter Scott's dramatic 1817 novel,* Rob Roy.

- **The Jacobites** defeated the English at Prestonpans, then invaded England, advancing as far as Derby before they lost their nerve and retreated.

- **In the sleet,** on bleak Culloden moor near Inverness on 16 April 1746, the Jacobites were routed by the English and lowland Scots under the Duke of Cumberland. Cumberland came to be called Butcher, because of the way he ruthlessly hunted down and killed survivors.

▼ *When Jacobites led by Bonnie Prince Charlie rose up in the 1740s, they were brutally crushed, at the bleak and bloody Battle of Culloden Moor, by England's Duke of Cumberland.*

Napoleon

- **Napoleon Bonaparte** (1769-1821) was the greatest general of modern times, creating for a short while a French empire that covered most of Europe.

- **Napoleon** was quite short (157 cm) and was nicknamed le Petit Caporal ('the tiny corporal'). But he was an inspiring leader, with a genius for planning and an incredibly strong will.

- **Napoleon** was born on the island of Corsica. At the age of nine he went to army school and joined the French army at fourteen.

- **The Revolution** gave Napoleon the chance to shine and by 1794, at just 25, he was a brigadier general.

▼ *The Battle of Waterloo, in 1815, was a hard-won conquest that finally ended Napoleon's bids for power. Leading the victors was British general Wellington, aided by the last-minute arrival of Prussian troops and some serious French errors.*

▶ *Napoleon, with his right hand hidden, characteristically, inside his jacket.*

- **In 1796,** days after marrying Josephine de Beauharnais, Napoleon was sent with a small troop simply to hold up the invading Austrians. Instead, he drove them back as far as Vienna and conquered much of Austria.

- **By 1804,** Napoleon's conquests had made him a hero in France, and he elected himself as Emperor Napoleon I.

- **By 1812,** Napoleon had defeated all the major countries in Europe but Britain and decided to invade Russia.

- **Napoleon's** invasion of Russia ended in such disaster that it broke his power in Europe. Soon afterwards, he was defeated at Leipzig, Paris was occupied by his enemies and he was sent into exile on the isle of Elba.

- **Napoleon escaped** from Elba in March 1815 to raise another army, but this was defeated by Wellington's armies at Waterloo, Belgium in June.

- **After Waterloo,** Napoleon was sent to the island of St Helena in the mid-Atlantic, where he died, aged 51.

Ireland

- **When the Irish high king,** Turlough O'Connor, overthrew Dermot, the king of Leinster, c.1160, Dermot asked Henry II, the Norman king of England, for help.

- **When Dermot died,** the Norman baron Strongbow made himself king of Leinster. Henry II invaded and Normans slowly gained control of all Ireland.

- **Norman English power** in Ireland weakened as many people adopted Irish ways. By the 1400s, they controlled only a small area round Dublin called the Pale.

  - **The phrase 'beyond the Pale'** originally meant the dark and wild Ireland outside the Pale.

  - **To regain** control, the English began the 'plantation of Ireland' – giving English settlers land there.

  - **In the late 1500s,** the English queen Elizabeth I tried to set up Protestantism in Ireland by force.

  - **The Irish** in Ulster revolted, led first by Shane O'Neill and later his nephew Hugh O'Neill, but Elizabeth crushed the rebellion in 1603.

◄ *Shane O'Neill, who led Irish revolts against Elizabeth I's attempts to force Ireland to accept Protestantism.*

- **Oliver Cromwell** stamped out another Irish revolt in 1649.

- **After the defeat** of James II at the Boyne, Irish Catholics lost more land to English and Irish Protestants. By 1704, they owned just fifteen per cent of Ireland.

- **In 1798,** Wolfe Tone led another Irish revolt – aided by a small French army – but the revolution was soon crushed.

▼ *In July, 1690, William III of England fought the former King James II for the English crown at the Battle of the Boyne in Ireland.*

Industrial unrest

- **Wages** in the new factories of the Industrial Revolution were low and working conditions were very poor.

- **Luddites** were English factory workers who, in 1811-12, smashed new machines that put people out of work.

- **High taxes** on imported corn meant that the poor were first to suffer in times of bad harvest, such as 1816-19.

- **The 'Peterloo' massacre** of 16 August 1819 was caused by a cavalry charge into a crowd gathered to hear radical leader Henry Hunt in Manchester's St Peter's field.

- **Welsh-born Robert Owen** (1771-1858) was the first great factory reformer and socialist.

▲ *Welshman Robert Owen did much to promote better conditions for workers.*

- **Owen set up** 'ideal' communities at New Lanark in Scotland and New Harmony in Indiana, USA, where people might work together in good conditions.

- **Trade unions** were banned by British 'Combination' Acts. But these were partly removed in 1824.

- **Owen's** Grand National Consolidated Trades Union of 1833 – the first national union – was instantly repressed by the government.

- **The Tolpuddle martyrs** were six Dorset farmworkers transported to Australia in 1834 for trying to form a trade union.

▲ *Sheffield, northern England in 1879 – one of Europe's major centres during the Industrial Revolution, famed for its steel production. Cities such as this became hot-beds of unrest among badly treated workers.*

FASCINATING FACT
Thomas Paine's radical book *The Rights of Man* (1792) was the inspiration for many protesters.

Austria and Prussia

◀ *As well as being a ruthless military leader, Frederick the Great played and composed flute music and exchanged long letters with the philosopher Voltaire.*

- **In 1711,** Austria, Hungary, Germany and parts of Italy were part of the Holy Roman Empire. The emperor was Charles VI, the Archduke of Austria.

- **Charles VI** had no sons, but wanted his young daughter Maria Theresa to rule after him.

- **When Charles VI died, in 1740,** three non-Austrians claimed they should be emperor. Maria Theresa rallied her Austrian people to defend her claim.

- **The War of the Austrian Succession** began with Britain, Hungary and the Netherlands backing Maria Theresa. Prussia, France, Bavaria, Saxony, Sardinia and Spain opposed her.

- **In 1742,** Maria Theresa was defeated and Charles of Bavaria became emperor. Charles, however, died in 1745. Maria Theresa's husband Francis I became emperor, though Maria was actually in charge.

- **The rise of Prussia** is linked to the rise of their ruling family the Hohenzollerns, and aristocratic landlords called junkers.

- **In 1417,** Frederick Hohenzollern became elector of Brandenburg. This meant he was one of the chosen few who could elect the Holy Roman Emperor.

- **By 1701,** Brandenburg expanded to become Prussia. Frederick I became its first king and built up its army.

- **Frederick I's son**, Frederick II or Frederick the Great (1712-86), was Prussia's greatest ruler. Frederick II was ambitious and manoeuvred Austria, France and Russia into wars that he used to gain land.

- **Austria and Prussia** lost much of their power after they were beaten by Napoleon's armies.

▶ *Maria Theresa's fight to become Holy Roman Emperor was crushed and Charles of Bavaria took the title. However, she rose to power once again as the wife of Charles's successor, Francis I.*

125

Napoleonic wars

- **The Napoleonic wars** were the long and bitter wars (1796-1815) between the France of Napoleon and other European countries, including Britain.

- **The wars began** with Napoleon's victories over the Austrians in Italy in 1796.

- **Napoleon** wanted to destroy British trade with the Middle East, and so attacked Egypt in 1798, defeating Egypt's rulers the Mamelukes. Napoleon's fleet was destroyed on the Nile by the British under Lord Nelson, but Napoleon then beat the Turks at Abuqir.

- **The French Revolution** had introduced a conscript system, which meant that every Frenchman had to serve in the army – Napoleon's army was 750,000 in 1799. Two million more had joined up by 1815.

- **In 1805,** Britain, Russia and Austria allied against Napoleon. Napoleon crushed the Austrians and Russians at Austerlitz. When Prussia joined Russia, Napoleon routed the Prussians at Jena and Auerstadt and the Russians at Friedland. But in 1805 Nelson's ships had destroyed the French and Spanish fleets at Trafalgar. Nelson died at Trafalgar, but his victory ended Napoleon's chances of invading Britain.

▼ *Napoleon's retreat from Moscow in 1812 was one of the worst military disasters. The winter trek was so cold and food so scarce, only 30,000 of the army of 695,000 that set out made it back to France. However, the biggest cause of death was the spread of the disease typhus.*

- **A key element** in the French success was the 'column'. Instead of advancing in a thin line, men marched almost up to the enemy in columns, then spread out.

- **Napoleon** tried to destroy Britain with the 'Continental System', which banned any country from trading with it.

- **In 1812,** Napoleon captured Moscow, but the Russians burned everything as they fell back – leaving the French without food.

▲ *This map shows some of the major battles of the Napoleonic Wars.*

- **After the 1812 disaster,** Napoleon's enemies moved in swiftly. After a defeat at Leipzig, Napoleon abdicated. His brief comeback in 1815 ended in defeat at Waterloo.

> **FASCINATING FACT**
> Napoleon won many victories by holding much of his army in reserve until he had opened up a carefully chosen weak point in enemy lines.

The year of revolutions

▲ *When rioters raged through Vienna, the feared Prince Metternich and many of his hated secret police were forced to flee.*

- **The year 1848** saw revolutions break out right across Europe – in France, Germany, Italy, Austria and Hungary.

- **The revolutions** were not linked directly, but the revolutionaries had many of the same grievances.

- **Most revolutionaries** were also angry at repressive governments in which too few had a say.

128

▶ *Karl Marx (1818-83), founder of international communism. The ground-breaking* Communist Manifesto *that he wrote with Engels appeared during the year of revolution – 1848.*

- **Many revolutionaries** were angry too at the poverty suffered by ordinary people in the new industrial cities.

- **Many places,** like Hungary, Germany and Italy, were under the power of a foreign government, and revolutionaries were often nationalists who wanted freedom from foreign oppression for their country.

- **In Paris,** revolutionaries shouting 'bread or death' stormed government buildings, threw out the king and set up a republic.

- **In Vienna,** the powerful Prince Metternich and emperor were forced to flee as people created their own parliament and freed serfs.

- **In Hungary,** revolutionary leader Louis Kossuth set up a short-lived Hungarian republic.

- **In London**, the last and biggest Chartist rally took place. The Chartists had a charter demanding votes for all men and other political reforms. The rally dispersed peacefully.

- **All but the Paris revolution** were quickly dealt with by armies – but the desire for change grew stronger over the century. The *Communist Manifesto*, written by Karl Marx and Friedrich Engels, was to become the basis of the great revolutions in Russia and China.

129

Latin American revolts

- **By 1800,** Latin Americans were ready to revolt against the centuries of rule by Spain and Portugal.

- **When the Napoleonic Wars** turned Spain and Portugal into a battleground, Latin American revolutionaries seized their chance.

- **Mexicans** led by priests Hidalgo and Morelos revolted in 1810. The Spanish quelled the revolt and executed Hidalgo and Morelos. In 1821, however, Mexico gained independence.

▼ *South Americans under Bolivar fought hard against the Spanish in modern-day Colombia and Peru.*

◀ *Simón Bolívar (1783-1830) was South America's greatest revolutionary hero, but as president of Gran Colombia he proved unpopular.*

- **In 1810,** José de San Martin led Argentina to independence. In 1816, San Martin made an epic march across the Andes to bring Chile freedom, too – with the help of Bernardo O'Higgins.

- **In the north,** Venezuelans Francisco de Miranda, Simón Bolívar and Antonio de Sucre led a long fight against the Spanish in New Granada (now Colombia) and Peru. In 1819, after a great victory at Boyaca in Colombia, Bolívar proclaimed the Republic of Gran Colombia (now Venezuela, Colombia, Ecuador and Panama).

- **In 1824,** Sucre won a crucial victory at Ayacucho in Peru, freeing all of north South America from Spanish rule.

- **The Republic** of Bolivia was named after Bolívar, who wrote its constitution. Sucre became its first president.

- **Brazil** gained its freedom from Portugal without a fight when its ruler Prince John fled. His son became emperor.

- **Miranda** died in a Spanish jail after Bolívar handed him over. Sucre was assassinated in 1830. Bolívar died in 1830, shortly after a failed assassination attempt.

> **FASCINATING FACT**
> In 1824, San Martin left for Europe, saddened by disputes after independence and his wife's death.

131

Italian independence

▲ *The glittering city of Venice became part of a united Italy in 1866.*

- **After the Napoleonic Wars,** Italy was split into various kingdoms – some, like Naples, under French Bourbon kings, some under Austrian rule and papal states under the pope.

- **The Carbonari** ('charcoal burners') were a secret society working for Italian freedom.

- **In 1820,** the Carbonari got the Bourbon king of Naples to agree to a constitution, but the Austrians intervened to abolish it.

- **In 1831,** Giuseppe Mazzini founded 'Young Italy' to unite Italy. The drive to unite the country became known as the *Risorgimento* ('rising again').

- **In 1848,** revolutions broke out across Italy, but were put down.

- **In 1857,** Count Cavour, prime minister of Piedmont, asked France for help with evicting the Austrians.

- **In 1859,** France and Piedmont beat the Austrians at Magenta and Solferino. After political wrangling, northern Italy was joined to Piedmont under King Victor Emmanuel II.

- **Magenta** was such a bloody battle that a new purple-red colour was named after it.

- **In 1860,** the great hero Garibaldi led a rebellion and conquered all of southern Italy. Only Cavour's intervention stopped Garibaldi from taking Rome.

- **In 1861,** most of Italy was united under Victor Emmanuel. Venice was added in 1866 and Rome as capital in 1870.

▶ *Garibaldi was the hero who landed in Italy with just his thousand famous 'Red Shirts'. He went on to conquer all of southern Italy.*

The Irish famine

- **The Irish potato famine** (1845-49) was one of the worst human disasters of the 1800s, when more than a million people in Ireland died of starvation.

- **In the 1800s**, most Irish were poor farmers, working tiny plots of land rented from Anglo-Irish landlords.

- **Potatoes were introduced** from America in the 1700s. They were such a successful crop that the Irish population grew to 8.4 million by 1844, but most were very poor.

- **Half the Irish** population depended entirely on potatoes for food, because English laws kept the price of bread too high for the poor Irish to buy.

- **In 1845,** much of the potato crop was ruined by blight, a disease caused by the fungus Phytophthora.

- **When the blight** ruined even more of the 1846-49 potato crops, millions of poor Irish farmers began to starve.

◀ *Potatoes became the staple food of the Irish poor because laws established by the English made bread too expensive.*

- **By August 1847,** three million were fed entirely on rations from soup kitchens set up by landlords and the British.

- **Many poor tenant farmers** were thrown off their land because they had no crop to sell in order to pay the rent.

- **Throughout the famine,** Irish farms exported grain, meat and vegetables too costly for the Irish to buy.

- **One and a half million** desperate Irish people packed up and left for America, leaving the country half-empty.

▼ *The potato famine devastated Ireland.*

135

The British Empire

- **At its height,** in 1920, the British Empire covered a quarter of the world and ruled a quarter of the world's population.

- **The British** ruled more peoples than any other nation.

- **The British Empire** began to build up in the 1600s, as British merchants started to extend their trading links throughout the world. The British won out over Dutch, Portuguese, French and Belgian rivals through the success of their navy and also their reasonably efficient colonial government.

- **The 13 American colonies** broke away in 1776, but Canada and many West Indian islands remained British.

- **Britain** gained control of India through the East India Company, between 1757 and 1858. In 1877, Queen Victoria was proclaimed Empress of India – the first time the word empire had been used in relation to the British possessions.

- **Many of the British possessions** had similar climates to Britain's – parts of Canada, South Africa, Australia and New Zealand – and British settlers moved to these places in huge numbers in the 1900s, pushing out the native inhabitants. These colonies were given more and more freedom to govern themselves and came to be called 'dominions'.

- **The Empire** reached its peak after World War 1, when German and Turkish possessions were added.

- **After World War 2,** more countries demanded independence. India and Pakistan became independent in 1947, Ceylon in 1948. By 1980, most African, West Indian and Pacific Island colonies were independent.

◀ *The British Empire was controlled by the British navy and army. The army worked in every continent, from India to Egypt, and Australia to Canada.*

● **Most colonies** remained within the Commonwealth after independence. There are 54 Commonwealth nations, linked essentially by agreed principles, but they all accept the British queen as head of the Commonwealth.

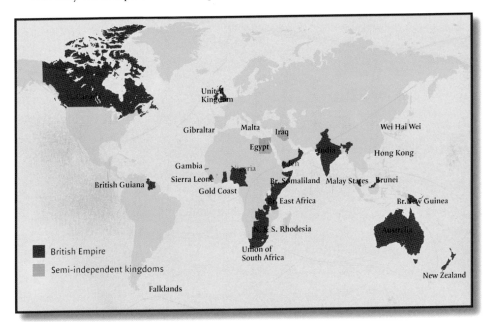

▲ *This map shows the British Empire in the 1930s, when it was beginning to shrink. Egypt was given some independence in 1922, when Sultan Ahmed became King Fuad I. Iraq gained a similar independence when amir Ahd Allah Faisal became King Faisal I.*

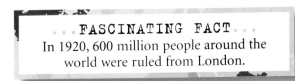

. . . . **FASCINATING FACT** . . . .
In 1920, 600 million people around the world were ruled from London.

The American Civil War

◀ *The Union flag had stars for all the 13 original states (top). The Confederates had their own version of the flag, also with 13 stars.*

● **The American Civil War** (1861-65) was fought between northern states (the Union) and southern states (the Confederacy). It split friends and families and killed over 600,000 Americans.

● **The main cause** was slavery. In 1850, slavery was banned in the 18 northern states, but there were 4 million slaves in the 15 southern states, where they worked on huge plantations.

● **The conflicts developed** over whether new states, added as settlers pushed westward, should be 'slave' or 'free' states.

● **In 1854,** slavers gained legal victories with the Kansas-Nebraska Act, which let new states decide for themselves.

● **In 1860,** the Abolitionist (anti-slavery) Republican, Abraham Lincoln, was elected as president.

● **The southern states** immediately broke away from the Union in protest, to form their own Confederacy.

- **As the war began,** the Confederates had the upper hand, fighting a defensive campaign.
- **The turning point** came in July 1863, when an invading southern army, commanded by Robert E Lee, was badly defeated at Gettysburg in Pennsylvania.
- **The extra** industrial resources of the north slowly began to tell and General Grant attacked the south from the north, while Sherman advanced ruthlessly from the west.
- **Lee surrendered** to Grant in Appomattox Court House, Virginia, on 9 April 1865. Slavery was abolished, but a few days later Lincoln was assassinated.

▼ *The American Civil War has been described as the very first 'modern war'. It was basically a fight between two different philosophies of life – the forward-thinking, industrial, anti-slavery north versus the old-fashioned pro-slavery south, with its greater military resources.*

Australia

- **In 1788,** the British sent a fleet of 11 ships, carrying convicts, to start a prison colony in Australia.

- **The fleet landed** at Botany Bay, but the first governor, Arthur Phillip, settled in a new site that eventually became the city of Sydney.

- **160,000 convicts** were sent to Australia over the next 80 years, but by 1810 British settlers were arriving voluntarily.

- **After 1850,** settlers set up vast sheep farms in the interior. Many Aborigines were killed as they fought for their land.

- **In 1851,** gold was discovered in New South Wales and Victoria and many thousands of people came to Australia to seek their fortune, tripling the population to 1.1 million in just nine years.

- **After the gold rushes,** ex-miners campaigned to 'unlock the lands' – that is, free up land from squatters and landowners for small farmers.

- **In the 1880s and 90s,** Australians began to become aware of their own national identity – partly as Australian cricketers became heroes – and demand self-government.

- **In 1901,** Australia became the independent Commonwealth of Australia, with its own parliament at Melbourne.

- **In 1927,** the Australian government moved to a new capital in Canberra.

- **In 2000,** Australians voted to keep the British queen as head of state, rather than become a republic.

▶ *Famous Yorkshire-born navigator James Cook (1728-79) sailed around the Pacific charting New Zealand, Australia and several island groups. Here he is seen on the Cook Islands (some way east of Australia, in Polynesia), which bear his name.*

The scramble for Africa

- **From 1500 to 1800,** Europeans were familiar only with the coast of Africa, from which slaves were taken.

- **After 1800,** many Europeans wanted to explore the interior in order to spread Christianity.

- **Some Europeans** wanted to develop trade in products like minerals and palm oil to help combat the slave trade.

- **Many European explorers,** such as David Livingstone and Richard Burton, went to Africa to find out more about its 'dark' (unknown) interior.

- **The wealth brought** to Britain by its colonies, such as India and North America, spurred the European powers to look for more lands to colonize.

▶ *Scottish missionary David Livingstone (1813-73) undertook several expeditions to Africa. Having gone missing while seeking the source of the Nile, he was famously 'found' by H M Stanley, in 1871.*

142

▶ *The European colonies in Africa and the dates they were acquired.*

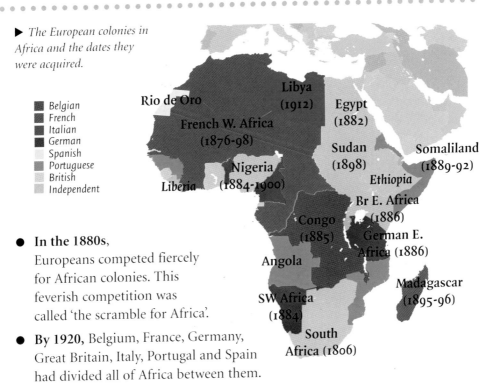

- **Belgian**
- **French**
- **Italian**
- **German**
- Spanish
- Portuguese
- British
- Independent

Rio de Oro

Libya (1912)

Egypt (1882)

French W. Africa (1876-98)

Sudan (1898)

Somaliland (1889-92)

Nigeria (1884-1900)

Ethiopia

Liberia

Br E. Africa (1886)

Congo (1885)

German E. Africa (1886)

Angola

Madagascar (1895-96)

SW Africa (1884)

South Africa (1806)

- **In the 1880s,** Europeans competed fiercely for African colonies. This feverish competition was called 'the scramble for Africa'.

- **By 1920,** Belgium, France, Germany, Great Britain, Italy, Portugal and Spain had divided all of Africa between them.

- **In some parts** of Africa, colonial rule was established peacefully by agreement with the Africans.

- **In Nigeria** and Ghana, the Africans fought hard against British rule, and in Tanzania and Namibia, they fought against German rule.

- **Ethiopia and Liberia** were the only countries in Africa to hold on to their independence.

143

The Oregon trail

- **After the USA** became independent, in 1783, waves of settlers began to move westward.

- **The first settlers** were fur traders. These were followed by cattle ranchers, then other farmers.

- **When cattle ranchers** moved to the Great Plains, they grazed huge herds on the open range and drove them to newly built rail depots for shipment east.

- **The cattle ranchers** of the Great Plains employed cowboys to herd the cattle and these cowboys became the symbol of the American west.

- **As the settlers** pushed west they came into conflict with Native Americans who already lived there.

- **The settlers** made many treaties with local peoples but broke almost all of them, and Native Americans were gradually driven from their lands or simply slaughtered.

- **In each decade,** new settlers struggled further west, facing great hardship in the hope of finding a new life.

- **Settlers** often set out with all their possessions in a covered wagon, often travelling with other wagons in a train (convoy) for safety.

- **The Oregon trail** was the longest of the routes to the west, winding over 3000 km from Independence, Missouri to the Pacific northwest.

- **The first group** of 900 wagons set out on the Oregon trail in the Great Migration of 1843.

▶ *Would-be settlers packed everything they owned in a covered wagon and joined a train of wagons heading west. They travelled in convoy for safety, as they were passing through, and staking claim to, land that had been inhabited by Native Americans for centuries.*

The Crimean War

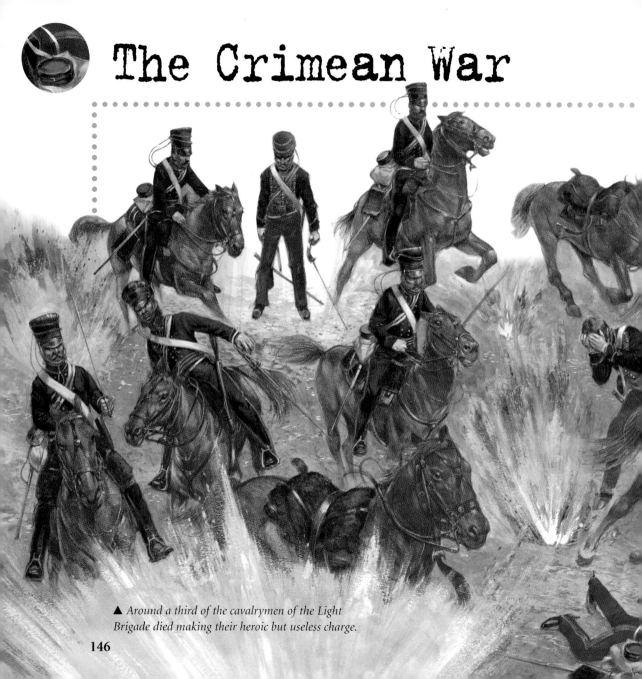

▲ *Around a third of the cavalrymen of the Light Brigade died making their heroic but useless charge.*

- **The Crimean War** was fought in the Crimea – to the north of the Black Sea – between 1854 and 1856.

  - **On one side** was Russia. On the other were Turkey, Britain, France, and Piedmont/Sardinia, while Austria gave political support.

    - **The main cause** of the war was British, French and Turkish worries about Russian expansion in the Black Sea.

      - **The war began** when Russia destroyed the Turkish fleet.

      - **Armies on both sides** were badly organized. Many British soldiers died of cholera before they even reached the Crimea and wounded soldiers suffered badly from cold and disease.

    - **During the Battle of Balaklava,** on 25 October 1854, a stupid mistake sent a gallant British cavalry charge straight on to the Russian guns. The heroic 'Charge of the Light Brigade' was made famous in a poem by Tennyson.

      - **Conditions** in the battle hospitals were reported in the first-ever war photographs and in the telegraphed news reports of W H Russell.

      - **Nurses** like Florence Nightingale and Jamaican Mary Seacole went to the Crimea to help the wounded.

        - **Lessons learned** in the Crimea helped to lay the foundations of modern nursing.

        - **The war** finally ended in 1856 with the Treaty of Paris, with few gains on either side.

147

Germany

- **In 1815,** Germany was divided among 38 different states of the German Confederation.

- **The most powerful** of the German states were Prussia and Austria, who sparred for dominance.

- **In 1862,** Otto von Bismarck (1815-98) became chancellor of Prussia. He was known as 'the Iron Chancellor ' and it was through his determination and skilful diplomacy that Germany was united.

- **In 1864,** Denmark tried to take over the disputed duchies of Schleswig and Holstein. The Austrians and Prussians sent an army to drive the Danes out.

- **Austria and Prussia** could not agree on what to do with Schleswig-Holstein.

- **Bismarck** proposed a new North German Confederation, excluding Austria.

- **Austria objected** to Bismarck's plan, but was defeated by Prussia in a very swift war in 1866.

- **To complete** Prussian control over Germany, Bismarck provoked a war against France, which had been the main opponent to German unity. He used the trick of the Ems telegram – a version of a telegram reporting a conversation between the Prussian king and the French ambassador, skilfully edited to imply an insult to France.

- **France** declared war on Prussia, but was swiftly beaten by the Prussians, who marched into Paris in January 1871.

- **After the defeat** of France, all the German states agreed to become part of a united Germany under Prussian leadership. On 18 January 1871, Wilhelm I was crowned kaiser (emperor).

 German Confederation

 North German Confederation 1866

 German Second Empire 1871

▲ *The North German Confederation was a union of states formed in 1867. Prussia dominated the confederation. Within this union, members were able to keep their own governments, but foreign and military policies were decided by a federal government.*

The rise of America

◄ *The president and Executive in the White House prepares laws and puts them into effect – and also conducts foreign affairs – but only Congress can make laws legal.*

- **In the late 1800s,** the USA changed from a nation of farming pioneers and plantation owners to the world's biggest industrial powerhouse. American inventors and industrialists made products that changed the world – the typewriter (1867), the telephone (1876), the phonograph (1877) and electric light (1879). Then, in the early 1900s, Henry Ford pioneered the mass production of cars and made cars affordable for millions of ordinary people.

- **The writer** Mark Twain called the era of industrialization 'the Gilded Age', to describe the culture of the newly rich. Without any traditions of their own to draw on, they developed a showy culture aping that of European aristocrats – going to operas and building enormous European-style mansions filled with antiques, works by European painters and rare books.

- **The less rich** enjoyed different kinds of show – circuses, vaudevilles and sport. By 1900, baseball was the national pastime. After 1920, motion pictures drew millions.

- **In the late 1800s,** people started to realize that American progress was leaving many behind, and reformers called Progressives began to demand change. In 1891, farmers and labourers formed the Populist party.

- **In 1903,** Theodore Roosevelt was elected as president and promised Americans a 'square deal'. He tried to curb the power of monopolies like Standard Oil and supported striking miners.

- **Until 1900,** the USA played little part in world affairs. Bismarck said, 'A special Providence takes care of fools, drunkards and the USA'. But in 1898, the US battleship *Maine* was blown up off Cuba. Americans blamed the Spanish and in the war that followed, the USA easily defeated Spain.

- **From 1900 on,** the USA became more and more involved in world affairs, stepping in later in both World War 1 and World War 2 to play a decisive role. By the late 1900s, the USA saw itself to some extent as the world's policeman.

- **By the 1920s,** America was booming. The 1920s were known as the 'Roaring Twenties', because the pace of change was so exciting, and cars and loud jazz music made the new America so noisy and vibrant.

- **The confidence** of the 1920s spurred wild speculation on money markets, and in 1929 New York's Wall Street stock market crashed. US economic power was now so great that the crash plunged the world into the Great Depression of the 1930s, which saw businesses fold and millions unemployed.

> **. . . FASCINATING FACT . . .**
> By 1930, Americans owned 23 million cars –
> three times as many as the rest of the world.

151

Victorian England

- **In 1837,** 18-year-old Victoria became the queen of England and reigned for 63 years until 1901 – the longest reign in British history.

- **Victoria's reign** is called the Victorian Age.

- **In the Victorian Age,** Britain became the world's largest industrial and trading power and the British Empire reached its peak.

- **British factories and towns** mushroomed and railways were built throughout the country.

- **In 1851,** the Great Exhibition opened in a huge building of glass and iron, later called the Crystal Palace, to show British skills to the world.

- **In 1861,** Victoria's husband, Prince Albert, died and she went into mourning and wore black the rest of her life.

▲ *Under Queen Victoria, Britain came to wield control over the largest empire the world had ever seen, and made astonishing artistic, scientific and manufacturing advances.*

▶ *Benjamin Disraeli, twice prime minister in Victorian England (1868 and 1874-1880), and one of Victoria's favourite statesmen. Under Disraeli, the British Empire gained even more status when Victoria became Empress of India.*

- **The rapid expansion** of Victorian cities created vast slum areas where living conditions were appalling.

- **Social reformers** and writers such as Charles Dickens highlighted the problems of the slums. Slowly, Parliament passed laws to improve conditions for working people and to provide education for all.

- **The two great** prime ministers of the Victorian Age were the flamboyant Benjamin Disraeli (1804-81) and the dour William Gladstone (1809-98).

- **Victorian middle-class life** cultivated cosy moral values, but there was also a seamy side, with widespread prostitution and crime.

The Balkans

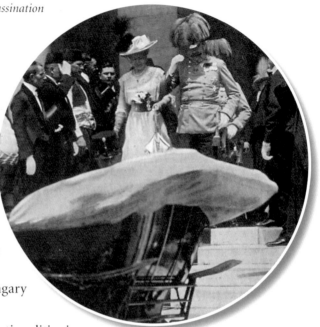

▶ *Within just four days after the assassination of Archduke Franz Ferdinand, World War 1 had started.*

- **The Balkans** are the countries of southeastern Europe. The word *balkan* is Turkish for 'mountain'.

- **In 1800,** people of many nationalities lived in the Balkans – Slovenes, Croats, Serbs, Bulgars, Greeks and Turks.

- **All the Balkan peoples** were ruled over by two old and weak empires – Austria-Hungary and Ottoman Turkey.

- **Through the 1800s,** many nationalities in the Balkans worked for independence.

- **European powers** like Russia and Germany encouraged independence movements for their own purposes.

- **Between 1829 and 1908,** Greece, Montenegro, Serbia, Romania and Bulgaria gained some independence, but many of their people were still within the old empires.

- **Austria refused** Slovenia and Croatia independence and held on to Bosnia-Herzegovina, which Serbia claimed.

154

- **In 1912,** various Balkan countries conspired to drive the Turks out of Europe in the First Balkan War, but rivalry between them led to a Second Balkan War in 1913, which let the Turks back in and left the Balkans highly unstable.

- **In June 1914,** Archduke Franz Ferdinand was assassinated in Sarajevo by Gavrilo Princip, a Serbian activist from Bosnia-Herzegovina.

- **Austria** believed Serbs were behind the assassination and declared war. Russia defended the Serbs as they had pledged by secret treaty. Soon all of Europe was engaged in World War 1.

▲ *Tanks first appeared in WW1. They were effective against gunfire, but often broke down.*

The Opium Wars

▲ *Millions of Chinese became addicted to opium in the early 1800s.*

- **From 1759 to 1842,** Chinese emperors let European merchants trade only in the port of Guangzhou, and buy tea and silk only from the cohong (guild) of Chinese firms.

- **To pay for Chinese goods,** the East India Company used opium, the drug made from poppies. Huge loads of opium grown in India were sold to Chinese drug dealers.

- **All the silver** used to pay for opium upset the Chinese economy and opium-smuggling got out of hand.

▶ *Opium is obtained from a certain type of poppy. It is made by drying an extract from seed capsules that have not yet ripened.*

- **In March 1839,** Chinese commissioner Lin Tse-hsü seized 20,000 crates of opium from British merchants.

- **Many ordinary** Chinese backed the British, because the British gave them opium and because the emperor's restrictive rule had brought poverty and hunger.

- **In 1840,** 16 British warships went to Guangzhou, starting the First Opium War. The Chinese were easily beaten.

- **Under the Treaty of Nanjing** in 1842, the Chinese gave Britain Hong Kong, abolished the cohong system and opened up trade to specially favoured nations.

- **In 1856,** Chinese police seized the *Arrow*, a ship flying a British flag, thus starting the Second Opium War.

- **British and French** armies invaded China and, after some wrangling, occupied Beijing in 1860.

- **At the Beijing Convention,** China opened more ports to western trade and allowed Europeans to travel inland.

Abraham Lincoln

- **Abraham Lincoln** (1809-65) was America's 16th, and possibly greatest, president. He led the Union through the Civil War and the freeing of slaves.

- **He was born** in a backwoods log cabin in Kentucky, to a poor family.

- **He never went** to school but a relative said, "I never seen Abe after twelve 'at he didn't have a book in his hand or his pocket" – often the Bible.

- **He became a lawyer,** known for shrewd common sense and honesty. His defence of Rock Island Bridge (on the Mississippi River) against shipping interests made him famous.

▲ *Lincoln was a tall, lanky man. His razor-sharp mind, calm manner and resolutely moral attitudes made him a hero to many Americans.*

- **Once elected** to Congress, he went on to win political fame as an opponent of slavery through debates over the Kansas-Nebraska Act, in the 1850s.

- **In 1860,** just before the start of the Civil War, between north and south, he was elected president – on the votes of the northern states alone.

▲ *From left: presidents Washington, Jefferson, Roosevelt, Lincoln, carved into Mt. Rushmore.*

- **On 1 January 1863,** Lincoln announced his Emancipation Proclamation, which freed all slaves.

- **In 1863,** after the terrible battle of Gettysburg, Lincoln made a famous speech called the Gettysburg Address, which summed up the spirit of democracy. In it he vowed that 'government of the people, by the people, for the people, shall not perish from the Earth.'

- **When the war** ended, in 1865, he made plans for peaceful reconciliation.

- **He was shot dead** at Ford's Theatre, Washington by John Wilkes Booth, a fanatical southerner.

159

The Second Empire

- **In the 1840s,** the poverty of workers in French towns inspired men like Proudhon and Fourier to devise socialist ideas for solving various social problems.

- **Political meetings** were banned, so agitators held banquets to press their demands for liberal reforms.

- **On 22 February 1848,** the government banned a huge banquet in Paris, provoking such protest and rioting that King Louis-Philippe was forced to abdicate.

- **After much wrangling,** a new popular assembly set up the Second Republic and Louis-Napoleon Bonaparte was elected president in a vote by all French men.

- **Louis-Napoleon** (1808-73) was the son of Napoleon's brother and his step-daughter Hortense. In his youth, he had been active in the Italian Carbonari.

◀ *Radical politicians came to the fore in the Empire.*

160

▶ *Louis-Napoleon, nephew of Napoleon I and ruler of the Second Empire.*

- **The Assembly** proved conservative and, in 1852, Louis-Napoleon curbed their powers and had himself made Emperor Napoleon III by popular vote. His rule is called the Second Empire.

- **Napoleon III** gave state aid to industry, banks and railroads. Industry boomed and France grew rich. French engineers became world-famous.

- **Napoleon III's** Spanish wife, Eugenie, set the Empire Style for beautiful, lavish fashions and decoration that was mimicked across Europe.

- **Gradually,** Napoleon's rule provoked more and more hostility among radicals, and France's defeat by Germany in 1871 led to his downfall.

> ....FASCINATING FACT....
> The famous boulevards of Paris, with their grand houses, were created on Napoleon III's orders.

161

The Russian Revolution

▲ *The tsar's grand Winter Palace at St Petersburg, seized by revolutionaries in 1917.*

- **In 1861,** Tsar Alexander II freed Russian serfs, but they stayed poor. In towns, factory workers were just as poor.

- **Unrest among** factory workers and peasants grew and by 1901 there were two revolutionary parties: Socialist Revolutionary (SRP) and Socialist Democrat (SDP).

- **In 1903,** the SDP split into Bolsheviks (extremist majority), led by Lenin, and Mensheviks (moderate minority).

162

▶ *Tsar Nicholas II and family, who were fatally shot by Bolsheviks in the aftermath of the Revolution.*

- **In 1905,** after Russia's disastrous war against Japan, workers and peasants rose in revolt and workers from arms factories set up the first soviets (workers' councils).

- **Tsar Nicholas II** was forced to set up a Duma (parliament) but soon began to ignore it.

- **In March 1917,** terrible losses among Russian soldiers in World War 1, plus hardship at home, provoked a revolution.

- **The first 1917** revolution is called the February Revolution, because this was the month in the old Russian calendar.

- **Tsar Nicholas** abdicated. Later, the Bolsheviks shot him and all his family at Ykaterinburg.

- **The SRP**, led by Kerensky, had the upper hand at first, but more soviets were set up and Bolseheviks gained support.

- **On 7 November** (25 October on the old calendar), the Bolsheviks seized the Winter Palace in St Petersburg. Lenin headed a new government, based in Moscow, and ended the war, while soviets took control of major cities.

World War I

- **World War I** (1914-18), the Great War, was the worst the world had seen (World War II would prove to be worse), killing 10 million troops.

- **The war was caused** by the rivalry between European powers in the early 1900s. The assassination of Franz Ferdinand in Sarajevo, Balkans, on 28 June 1914 made Austria start a war with Serbia. Russia came to Serbia's defence. Germany declared war on Russia and her ally France on 3 August.

- **The Germans** had a secret plan (the 'Schlieffen plan') for invading France. Instead of tackling the French head-on, as expected, they swept round to the north through neutral Belgium. This outrage drew Britain into the war.

- **As the Germans** moved into France, they came up against the British and French (the Allies). The opposing armies dug trenches – and stayed facing each other in much the same place for four years. The trenches, known as the Western front, stretched from the English Channel to Switzerland.

- **The war soon** developed an Eastern front, where the Central Powers (Austria and Germany) faced the Russians. The deaths of millions of Russians provoked the 1917 Revolution, which took Russia out of the war.

- **In the Alps** the Central Powers were opposed by Italy. At Gallipoli in Turkey, British and Anzac (Australia and New Zealand) troops fought the Turks.

- **The Allies** relied on supplies from N. America, so the Germans used submarines to attack ships. The sinking of the *Lusitania* in May 1915, with 128 Americans out of 1198 casualties, brought the USA into the war.

- **In 1918** there were 3.5 million Germans on the Western front and in March they broke through towards Paris.

- **In July** British tanks broke the German line at Amiens.

- **An Allied naval blockade** meant many people were starving in Germany. As more US troops arrived, the Germans were pushed back. At 11 o'clock on 11 November 1918, the Germans signed an armistice (peace).

◀ *Trenches were dug to protect troops from enemy gunfire, but became hell-holes, filled with water, rats and disease. Soldiers had to eat, sleep and stand guard ankle-deep in mud. Every now and then, they were ordered to 'go over the top' – climb out of their trenches and advance towards enemy lines. Out of the trench, they were exposed to enemy fire, and quickly mown down. Millions of soldiers on both sides died. On 1 July 1916, 60,000 British soldiers were killed in just a few hours in the Battle of the Somme. The four-month Somme offensive killed 600,000 Germans, 400,000 British and 200,000 French – and advanced the Allies 7 km. The horror of war was conveyed in letters and poems by soldiers such as Siegfried Sassoon and Wilfred Owen.*

The Ottoman Empire

- **In 1774,** the Turkish Ottoman Empire was defeated by the Russians after a six-year war, and was forced to allow Russian ships to pass through the Straits from the Black Sea to the Mediterranean.

- **During the 1800s,** the Ottoman Empire grew weaker and weaker and was called 'the Sick Man of Europe' by foreign statesmen.

- **In 1829,** the Greeks fought a successful war of independence against the Turks. Other Balkan states followed suit.

- **During the 1800s,** the Turks fought four wars against Russia and lost three. Russia gained Bessarabia (now Moldova and Ukraine) and control of the Black Sea.

- **Trying to stop** the empire's decline, Sultan Abdul-Hamid II crushed opposition violently in the 1890s.

- **The Young Turks** were students and army officers who, in 1908, revolted against Abdul-Hamid and then ruled through his brother Muhammad V.

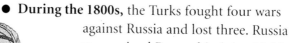

◀ *A sumptuously dressed Ottoman pasha, or high-ranking official (centre), with his noblemen.*

166

- **The Turks** joined World War 1 on the German side to regain territory lost to the Russians and in the Balkans.

- **After World War 1** ended, the Allies invaded Turkey and broke up the empire, leaving just modern Turkey.

- **The nationalist hero** Mustafa Kemal became first president of the Turkish republic, on 29 October 1923.

- **Kemal** became known as Ataturk (father of the Turks). He created modern Turkey by reforming education, law and languages.

▶ *This mosque is a fine example of architecture from the early Ottoman period.*

The rise of the Nazis

- **Even before** World War 1 ended, Germans had risen in revolt against their kaiser (emperor), Wilhelm II.

- **Wilhelm II** was driven out and in 1919 Germany became a republic, with a president elected by the people.

- **The republic** was called the Weimar Republic, because that was where the constitution had been drafted.

▲ *To boost their support, the Nazis held huge meetings called rallies, at which their cross symbol, the swastika, was prominently displayed.*

- **Under the peace terms** for World War 1, Germany was forced to pay huge amounts of money for war damage.

- **The cost of the war** ruined the German economy and rapidly rising prices made people poor overnight.

- **In 1923,** the National Socialist German Workers Party – Nazis – led by Adolf Hitler, tried a rebellion in Munich. The rebellion failed, but support for the Nazis grew.

- **The Great Depression** threw 6 million people out of work, and in 1933 enough people voted for the Nazis to make them the strongest party. Hitler became chancellor and set about destroying the opposition.

- **The Nazis** asserted German superiority over other races, including Jews and Slavs. They removed Jews from all government jobs and took away their rights.

- **On 9 Nov 1938,** Nazis broke windows and burned down synagogues and Jewish businesses. This night became known as *Kristallnacht* ('Night of the Broken Glass').

- **The Nazis** prepared for war to give Germans *Lebensraum* ('living space'). In 1936, they marched into the Rhineland. In 1938, they took Austria, followed by Czechoslovakia in 1939, and then Poland.

▲ *The dramatic collapse of the German economy caused by World War 1 and the Great Depression made the country's currency virtually worthless. Here, a girl is playing with large bundles of Mark notes, using them as building blocks.*

Lenin and Stalin

- **Lenin** (1870-1924) was the leader of the Communist revolution in Russia.

- **Lenin's real name** was Vladimir Ilyieh Ulyanov. He took the name Lenin from the River Lena in Siberia when he became a revolutionary.

- **Like Karl Marx** (1818-83), Lenin believed the world's workers would revolt and take over industry. Unlike Marx, he thought a small band of professionals like the Bolsheviks would need to lead the way.

- **After the 1905** revolution, Lenin lived in exile, but he returned to Russia when the tsar fell, in 1917.

- **After the October revolution,** Lenin ruled the country as head of the Bolsheviks (now the Communists). The Communists won the civil war that followed and in 1922 changed the Russian empire into a new nation, called the Union of Soviet Socialist Republics (USSR).

- **Joseph Stalin** (1879-1953) became dictator of the USSR after Lenin died in 1924, and remained so until he himself died, in 1953.

- **Stalin** was from Georgia and his real name was Joseph Vissarionovich Dzhugashvili.

▲ *Lenin and Stalin in rare agreement.*

- **Stalin used terror** to wipe out opposition and ensure the revolution survived. Russians lived in fear of the secret police NKVD (later the KGB), led by Beria, and millions went to their deaths in the Gulags (prison camps).

- **Millions of Russian peasants** starved in the 1930s as Stalin forced through government control of farms.

- **Stalin's** industrial programme transformed the USSR into one of the world's great industrial and military powers.

▼ *Lenin's tomb, in Red Square, Moscow. Over the years, countless thousands have queued up to see the embalmed body inside.*

Hitler

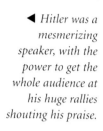

- **Adolf Hitler** (1889-1945) was the dictator who turned Germany into a war machine that started World War 2 and murdered 6 million Jews in the Holocaust.

- **Hitler** was born in Braunau-Am-Inn, Austria. A failed artist, he painted postcards before joining the German army in World War 1.

- **Hitler** was so angry at the terms ending World War 1 that he joined the National Socialist (Nazi) party, becoming its leader.

- **In 1923,** Hitler was put in prison after a failed Nazi coup, and there he wrote *Mein Kampf* ('My Struggle').

- **Mein Kampf** says Germany's problems were caused by Jews and communists and that it needed a strong führer (leader).

◄ *Hitler was a mesmerizing speaker, with the power to get the whole audience at his huge rallies shouting his praise.*

- **As the Depression** hit Germany in the early 1930s, Hitler's ideas gained support. In the 1933 elections, the Nazis got 37% of the vote and President Hindenburg asked Hitler to become chancellor (chief minister).

- **The Nazis** established the Gestapo (secret police) and used them to wipe out all opposition. When Hindenburg died in 1934, Hitler made himself führer.

- **Hitler** built up Germany's army, rigidly organized all workers and sent millions of Jews to concentration camps.

- **In 1938,** Hitler invaded Austria, then in 1939 Czechoslovkia and Poland too, and so began World War 2.

- **Finally,** as Germany faced defeat in 1945, he married his mistress Eva Braun on 29 April, in their bomb shelter in Berlin. They shot themselves the next day.

◀ *The worst of the Nazi concentration camps, such as Auschwitz, in Poland, became brutal death-centres. Millions of Jews were killed in these camps, many of them sent to horrific 'gas chambers', where they were poisoned with toxic gas.*

173

The Spanish Civil War

- **In the 1920s,** a weak economy and political unrest led General de Rivera to run Spain as dictator, alongside King Alfonso XIII.

- **In 1930,** the army drove Rivera out. In 1931, a popular vote for a republic persuaded Alfonso to leave Spain.

- **Spain** was split. On the Left were socialists, communists and ordinary people who supported the republic. On the right were wealthy landowners, army officers, the Catholic Church, and the fascist Falange party, who wanted the king back.

▲ *General Franco, victor of the Civil War and right-wing dictator of Spain for almost 40 years.*

- **Complicating the picture** were Catalonians and Basques, who wanted to break away from Spain.

- **In February 1936,** elections put the Popular Front, formed by all the left-wing groups, in power.

- **In July 1936,** a wave of army revolts started in Morocco and threatened to topple the Popular Front. The Popular Front supporters armed themselves and a bitter civil war began, with terrible atrocities on both sides.

- **The forces of the Right** were called the Nationalists and were led by General Franco. They were supported by fascist (very right-wing) Germany and Italy.

174

- **The forces of the Left** were called the Republicans or Loyalists and were supported by Soviet Russia. Liberals from other countries, like the writer Laurie Lee, formed an International Brigade to fight for the Loyalists.

- **At first,** Loyalists held the northeast and the big cities, but they gradually fell back. In March 1939, Franco's forces captured Madrid, the last Loyalist stronghold.

- Franco was dictator of Spain until he died in 1975.

▲ *A recruiting poster for the fascist Falange party.*

175

The Long March

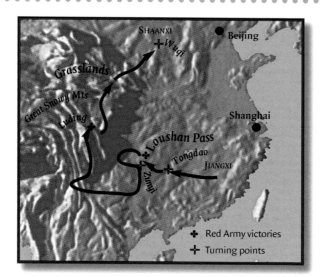

◀ *The heroic Long March of the Red Army – to escape the Nationalists – became the stuff of Chinese legend.*

- **In 1912,** the last Chinese emperor, six-year-old Pu-Yi, gave up his throne in the face of rebellion, and China became a republic, led by Sun Yat-sen.

- **When Sun** died, in 1925, leadership of his Kuomintang (Nationalist) party fell to Chiang Kai-shek, who allied with Communists to defeat warlords in the north.

- **In 1927,** Chiang Kai-shek turned on the Communists and forced their leaders to flee to the Jiangxi hills as he took control in Beijing.

- **By 1931,** the Communists had regrouped enough to set up a rival government in the south, called the Jiangxi soviet.

- **In 1934,** Chiang Kai-shek launched a massive attack on the Communist Red Army, forcing them to begin their famous Long March to the north to escape.

176

- **On the Long March,** the Red Army wound 10,000 km through the mountains, covering up to 100 km a day, until they reached Shaanxi in the north a year later.

- **Almost 95,000** of the 100,000 who set out on the Long March died of cold and hunger on the way. But, crucially, the Red Army survived.

- **During the March**, Mao Zedong became the Red Army leader.

- **Chiang** was forced to join with Mao to fight Japan in World War 2, and Mao built up Red Army forces.

- **After the war**, Mao drove the weakened Kuomintang out and took control. Chiang fled to Taiwan.

▶ *Pu-Yi, the last emperor of China before rebellion made the country a republic.*

World War II

- **World War II** (1939-45) was the most terrible war ever fought. It not only killed 17 million soldiers – compared to 10 million in World War I – but also twice as many civilians, through starvation, bombings and massacres.

- **It was the first** truly global war – fought on the plains of Europe, in the jungles of Southeast Asia, on the deserts of Africa, among the islands of the Pacific, on (and under) the Atlantic Ocean, and in many other places.

- **It began** when Hitler's Germany invaded Poland on 1 September 1939. Great Britain thought the USSR would defend Poland but Hitler and Stalin made a pact. As Germany invaded Poland from the west, the USSR invaded from the east.

'Never in the field of human conflict have so many owed so much to so few' – Churchill on the British fighter pilots.

- **After a lull,** or 'Phoney War', in May-June 1940, the Germans quickly overran Norway and Denmark, then Luxembourg, the Netherlands, Belgium and France.

- **The British army** was trapped by the Channel coast, but the Germans held back, and 338,000 British troops got away from Dunkirk, France, on an armada of little boats.

▶ *Winston Churchill (1874-1965) was the British prime minister whose courage and inspiring speeches helped the British withstand the German threat.*

▶ *The bombing of Pearl Harbour by the Japanese forced the US to enter the war. Almost 4000 people were killed or injured by the attack, with the main targets being US war ships.*

- **By August 1940,** Italy joined the war on the German side, and Germany launched air raids on England to prepare for an invasion. This was the Battle of Britain (above).

- **Fearing the USSR** would turn against him, Hitler launched a sudden invasion of the USSR on 22 June 1941. The USA joined the war when Japan bombed its fleet without warning in Pearl Harbor, Hawaii, on 7 Dec 1941.

- **Germany, Italy, Japan** and six other nations joined forces as the 'Axis'. Britain, the USA, USSR, China and 50 other nations were together called the Allies. In 1942, the Allies halted the Axis in Africa, invading Italy in 1943 and France in 1944. In 1945, the Allies drove into Germany from east and west. Germany surrendered on 7 May 1945. The terrible Pacific conflict ended when the USA dropped atom bombs on the Japanese cities Hiroshima and Nagasaki. Japan surrendered on 2 Sept 1945.

- **As the Allies** moved into Germany, they found the horror of Nazi death camps like Auschwitz and Buchenwald, where millions of Jews and others had been slaughtered by starvation and in gas chambers.

FASCINATING FACT
The key to the early German successes was the Blitzkrieg ('lightning war') – a stunningly rapid attack with tanks and aeroplanes.

India

- **Indian discontent** with British rule began to boil after the British killed 379 protestors at Amritsar, in 1920.

- **In 1920,** Mahatma Gandhi became the leader of a movement demanding independence for India.

- **Gandhi** led a series of non-violent protests against the British, such as boycotting British goods and refusing to pay taxes. He gained millions of supporters.

- **In 1930,** Gandhi marched to the sea to make salt from seawater in protest against a tax on salt.

- **In 1935,** the British gave India a new constitution that allowed Indians more power. For the Muslims, however, led by Mohammed Ali Jinnah, this was not enough.

- **Jinnah** demanded a new country for Muslims called Pakistan, separate from the Hindus.

- **In World War 2**, Indians said they would only fight on the British side if they were given independence.

- **In 1942,** Gandhi launched his 'Quit India' campaign to get rid of the British, who then jailed Indian leaders.

- **In 1946,** Britain offered independence to all of India, but Muslims did not want to live under a Hindu majority and terrible riots broke out in Calcutta.

- **Indian and British** leaders agreed to partition (split) India and Pakistan. Pakistan became independent on 14 August 1947, India the next day. 7.5 million Muslims immediately fled to Pakistan and 10 million Hindus to India.

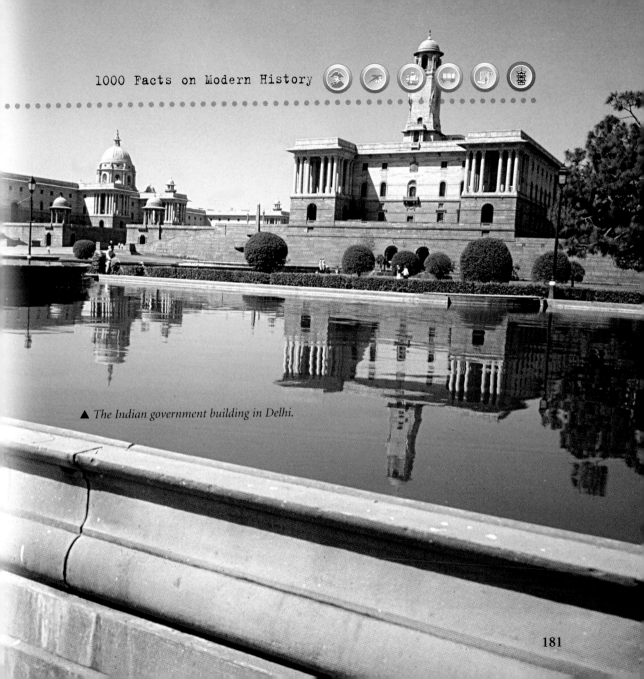

▲ *The Indian government building in Delhi.*

Mao

- **Mao Zedong** (1893-1976) led China's struggle towards communism and was China's leader for 27 years.

- **Mao was** born in 1893 to a poor peasant family in Shaoshan in Hunan.

- **In 1921,** he and 11 others formed the Chinese Communist Party. As support grew, Mao taught peasants guerilla tactics. He led the Red Army on the Long March.

◀ *The 'Little Red Book', properly called* The Thoughts of Chairman Mao, *became the bible of communist China.*

- **Mao** led the communist takeover of China in 1949 and then ruled China as chairman of the republic. Chinese people hoped communism would end poverty and oppression. 'We have stood up,' Mao said.

- **Mao** spurred peasants to turf out landlords and work together on collective farms. Peasants who had starved in the war ate again. Healthcare and education improved.

- **Mao's** ideas were stated in a little red book – *The Thoughts of Chairman Mao* – learned by heart by Chinese children.

- **In 1957,** Mao's 'Great Leap Forward' forced his people to work on communes to develop farming and industry. The upheaval brought famine and economic disaster.

- **In 1959,** Mao retired as chairman, but stayed in control.

- **In 1966,** Mao launched a 'Cultural Revolution' to purge China of corrupting foreign ideas. Led by Mao's wife Jiang Qing and friends (the Gang of Four), Mao's enemies were killed and scholars were tortured and imprisoned.

- **Mao died** in 1976 and the Gang of Four were driven out.

▶ *Mao's picture taking pride of place at the Forbidden City, Beijing – a walled medieval palace that was once home to China's long line of emperors.*

183

Gandhi

- **Mohandas Gandhi** (1869-1948) was the inspirational leader who led India's fight for independence in a remarkable campaign of non-violent protest.

- **Gandhi** is often called Mahatma, which means 'Great Soul'. He believed truth could only be known through tolerance and concern for others.

- **He was born** in Probandar in India. At 13, he married a girl of 13 called Kasturbai. They later had four children. At 19 he went to study law in London.

- **Gandhi** went to work as a lawyer in South Africa in 1893, but soon after arriving was thrown out of a railway carriage because of the colour of his skin. He then stayed in South Africa for 21 years to fight for Indian rights.

▶ *Gandhi always dressed with extreme simplicity, wearing just a plain robe and shorts, his feet bare or in sandals.*

▶ *A gathering of Indian Hindus. Gandhi campaigned to stop conflict between Hindus and Muslims.*

- **Gandhi** emphasized non-violent protest. By imposing hardship on himself and showing no anger or hatred, he believed he could persuade his opponents he was right. This method of action was called *Satyagraha*.

- **Gandhi** returned to India in 1915, and after the Amritsar massacre led India's fight for independence.

- **In 1920,** Gandhi began a programme of hand-spinning and weaving that he believed would give Indians economic independence, so challenging the British.

- **Gandhi** was jailed again and again for his protests, both in South Africa and India, and spent seven years in jail.

- **Gandhi** was assassinated on 30 January 1948, by a Hindu who hated his tolerance of Muslims and others.

. . . FASCINATING FACT . . .
In 1948, Gandhi persuaded Hindus and Muslims to stop fighting by going on a fast.

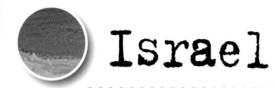

Israel

- **In the 1920s,** Palestine was under British rule, and the British encouraged Jews to settle there.

- **In the aftermath** of the Holocaust, when Hitler killed 6 million Jews, most countries supported the idea of a homeland where Jews would be free from persecution.

- **In 1948,** the United Nations split Palestine between Arabs and Jews. Arabs saw this as a theft of Arab land.

▲ *The Suez Canal, linking the Mediterranean and the Red Sea, was closed by Egypt during the 1967 war.*

- **Arabs immediately** invaded Israel (Jewish Palestine), but were defeated. Israel took over all of Palestine except the Gaza strip (to Egypt) and the West Bank (to Jordan).

- **In 1956-57,** Arab Egypt took control of the Suez Canal.

- **In 1967,** Egypt closed the Gulf of Aqaba, Israel's only way to the Red Sea. Israel declared war on the Arab states.

- **Israel** won the war in just six days, and calls it the 'Six Day War'. Arabs call it the 'June War'. Afterwards, Israel controlled Sinai, the Gaza strip and the West Bank.

- **In 1973,** Egypt attacked the Israelis in Sinai, starting the Yom Kippur War. With US help, the Israelis repulsed them.

- **By the Camp David Accords** of 1978, Egypt recognized Israel's right to exist and Israel returned Sinai to Egypt. US president Jimmy Carter set up the agreement.

- **The PLO,** led by Yasser Arafat, began to fight for Palestinian independence after the Six Day War. Fighting and negotiation continue to this day.

▼ *The mountainous, arid peninsula of Sinai has been fought over by Israel and Egypt for many years.*

The Cold War

- **The Cold War** was the rivalry between communist and non-communist countries after World War 2 – between the USSR and USA in particular.

- **It was called** the Cold War because the USSR and USA did not fight directly. But both supported countries that did – like the USA in Vietnam and the USSR in Korea.

- **The Iron Curtain** was the barrier between western Europe and communist eastern Europe.

- **The name Iron Curtain** was used by German propagandist Goebbels and adopted by Churchill.

- **The Berlin Wall** dividing communist East Berlin from the West was a powerful Cold War symbol. Dozens were shot trying to escape from the East over the wall.

◀ For many, the tearing down of the Berlin Wall, in 1989, marked the end of the Cold War. Berliners had a huge party on the ruins.

▶ *Fidel Castro, prime minister of Cuba at the time of 1962's missile crisis. The politics of Cuba's socialist revolutionary government was supported by the USSR and opposed by the USA.*

- **The Cold War** was fought using both propaganda and art and by secret means such as spies and secret agents.

- **The USA and USSR** waged an arms race to build up nuclear bombs and missiles one step ahead of their rival.

- **Real war** loomed when US president Kennedy threatened the USSR as it tried to build missile bases on Cuba in 1962.

- **The Cold War** thawed after 1985, when Soviet leader Mikhail Gorbachev introduced reforms in the USSR and began to co-operate with the West.

- **In 1989,** the Berlin Wall came down. In 1989-90, many eastern European countries broke away from Soviet control.

Scandinavia

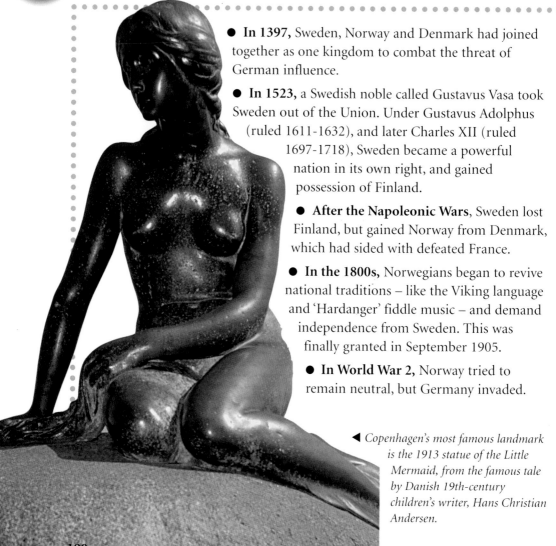

- **In 1397,** Sweden, Norway and Denmark had joined together as one kingdom to combat the threat of German influence.

- **In 1523,** a Swedish noble called Gustavus Vasa took Sweden out of the Union. Under Gustavus Adolphus (ruled 1611-1632), and later Charles XII (ruled 1697-1718), Sweden became a powerful nation in its own right, and gained possession of Finland.

- **After the Napoleonic Wars,** Sweden lost Finland, but gained Norway from Denmark, which had sided with defeated France.

- **In the 1800s,** Norwegians began to revive national traditions – like the Viking language and 'Hardanger' fiddle music – and demand independence from Sweden. This was finally granted in September 1905.

- **In World War 2,** Norway tried to remain neutral, but Germany invaded.

◄ *Copenhagen's most famous landmark is the 1913 statue of the Little Mermaid, from the famous tale by Danish 19th-century children's writer, Hans Christian Andersen.*

▲ *The flag of the EU (European Union). Denmark joined the EU in 1973 and Sweden in 1995.*

- **The Germans** made a Norwegian who helped them, Vidkun Quisling, prime minister. Quisling is now a word for traitor.

- **Since 1932,** Sweden has been governed mostly by the socialist SDP, who have spread Sweden's high standard of living to all levels of society.

- **In 1966,** the National Insurance Act passed by Norway's Storting (parliament) gave Norwegians one of the world's best welfare systems.

- **In 1986,** Swedish PM Olof Palme was assassinated.

- **Although Sweden and Denmark** joined the European Union, Norwegians voted against joining in 1994.

Japan

- **In 1942,** Japanese conquests in World War 2 gave it a huge empire across SE Asia, but after they lost the decisive naval battle of Midway to the USA, the tide turned against Japan.

- **The final blow** for the Japanese was the devastating atomic bombs dropped on the cities of Hiroshima (6 August 1945) and Nagasaki (9 Aug).

- **The Japanese** surrendered to the USA on 14 August 1945.

- **The surrender** brought a foreign occupying force to Japan, led by US general, Douglas MacArthur.

- **MacArthur** drew up a new constitution for Japan. Under this, Emperor Hirohito lost all real power.

▲ *Emperor Hirohito (1901-89) was the first Japanese emperor to give up his god-like status, ruling after 1945 as a figurehead only.*

- **The Americans** shared out farmland, legalized unions and improved women's and children's rights.

- **The occupation force** left in 1952.

- **Led by the government,** Japan recovered from the ruin of the war and launched itself on an amazing industrial boom which turned Japan into the world's healthiest economy in barely 25 years.

192

- **Japanese** society changed as people moved to the cities and the young began to behave independently.

- **In the 1980s,** the government was rocked by corruption scandals. The economy suffered too, as exports declined, and the country experienced a crisis of confidence.

▼ *The devastating atomic blast at Hiroshima killed or wounded around 150,000 people.*

South Africa

▲ *Under the harsh rules of apartheid, blacks and whites were 'segregated' – kept apart from each other – in all kinds of public places and situations.*

- **In 1910,** four British colonies – Transvaal, Orange Free State, Cape Colony and Natal – joined to make the self-governing Union of South Africa.

- **White people** had almost complete power in the Union, and blacks had virtually no legal rights.

- **Gandhi** campaigned for Indian rights in South Africa and had limited success.

- **When Gandhi** returned to India, black South Africans set up their own campaign in 1912 with the movement later called the ANC (African National Congress).

- **Afrikaners** – descended from the Dutch Boer people – began to fight for control. Their National Party made headway and in 1948 came to power. It enacted 'apartheid' laws to keep all the races firmly apart.

▶ *Nelson Mandela, South Africa's first black president. During his decades of imprisonment, Mandela provided a charismatic focus for ANC campaigns to end apartheid.*

- **The ANC** fought against apartheid – and especially against 'pass' laws that meant blacks had to carry passes.

- **In 1960,** police opened fire on protesting blacks at Sharpeville, killing 69. The government banned the ANC.

- **In the 1970s and 80s,** opposition to apartheid grew both in and outside South Africa, with many countries applying sanctions (trade restrictions).

- **In 1990,** President de Klerk released Nelson Mandela, an activist jailed since 1962, and repealed apartheid laws.

- **In 1994,** the ANC won the first open elections and Nelson Mandela became South Africa's first black president.

United Nations

- **In the aftermath** of World War 1, the great powers had set up a League of Nations – a forum for nations to come together, discuss world problems and so avoid war.

- **In 1942,** the Allies pledged to fight against the Axis powers with a statement called the Declaration by United Nations.

- **In 1944,** the same nations – including Britain, the USA, USSR and China – got together at Dumbarton Oaks in Washington DC to try and set up a peacekeeping organization.

- **The key to the** Dumbarton Oaks plan was a Security Council in which Britain, the USA, USSR and China would be permanent members.

- **In February 1945,** US president Roosevelt, British PM Churchill and Soviet leader Stalin met at Yalta in the Crimea and announced that a UN conference would meet in San Francisco. The three introduced the idea of them having a special veto (right to reject UN measures).

- **50 nations** met at San Francisco in April 1945 to draw up the Charter for the United Nations.

◀ *The UN flag flies over its permanent headquarters in New York.*

- **The Big Three** – Britain, the USA and USSR – gave themselves veto power over the Security Council, but the smaller nations gave the UN a General Assembly to help make it a truly global organization.

- **The UN Charter** came into effect on 24 October 1945.

- **In 1971,** the UN expelled Taiwan and admitted Communist China instead.

- **In recent years,** the UN peacekeeping force has been involved in keeping the peace in many places, including Somalia, Rwanda, Kosovo, Sierra Leone and E. Timor.

▼ *Churchill, Roosevelt and Stalin (from left) established the UN at their Yalta Conference, in 1945.*

197

Vietnam

- **From 1883,** Vietnam, along with Cambodia and Laos, was ruled by France as French Indochina or Indochine.

- **As Germany** invaded France in World War 2, Japan took over Vietnam.

- **When Japan** lost, in 1945, Vietnamese communists – the Vietminh, led by Ho Chi Minh – took over Vietnam.

- **British and Chinese** troops reclaimed Vietnam for the French, but the Vietminh fought back. The French set up a State of Vietnam under Bao Dai to oppose the Vietminh.

▲ *Ho Chi Minh, leader of the communist Vietminh.*

- **In 1954,** the warring parties agreed to split Vietnam into the North under Ho Chi Minh and South under Bao Dai.

- **The Vietminh-backed** Viet Cong started a rebellion in the South. In 1965, the USA began to bomb North Vietnam, while the USSR and China gave them arms.

- **As fighting escalated,** Americans began to protest against US involvement and in 1973, the US withdrew.

- **In 1975,** the Viet Cong captured Saigon, the capital of the South, and the next year united North and South.

- **One million** Vietnamese left as refugees, but by 2000, Vietnam was developing quietly and some returned.

▶ *US helicopters proved highly effective in the Vietnam jungles.*

FASCINATING FACT
The Vietnamese war was the first war that was widely televised as it happened.

Iraq and Iran

- **Iran** used to be called Persia, which, 2500 years ago, ruled over one of the great ancient empires.

- **The last shah** (king) of Iran, Muhammad Reza, although backed by the USA, was forced to flee the country in 1979 by Islamic extremists, led by the ayatollah (religious leader), Khomeini.

- **Iraq** used to be called Mesopotamia and was part of the Turkish Ottoman Empire until 1921 when it came under British control.

- **In 1930,** Britain promised Iraq independence. But British influence remained crucial until the last king, Faisal I, was killed and Iraq became a republic in 1958.

- **After years** of wrangling, Saddam Hussein became Iraqi president in 1979.

- **Saddam Hussein** was worried by the unsettling effects of the Islamic revolution in Iran and was also eager to regain some disputed territory.

- **In September 1980,** Iraq invaded Iran to begin the eight-year-long Iran-Iraq War.

◀ *Ayatollah Khomeini – Iran's head of state, 1979-89. He led a revolution in Iran that saw a return to very strict Islamic principles.*

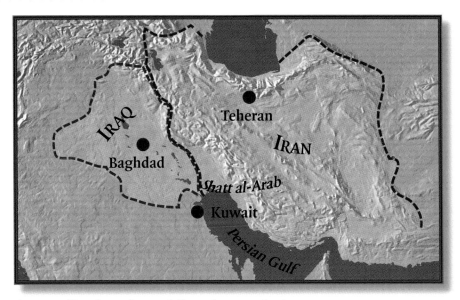

▲ *Iran and Iraq have a long and disputed common border.*

- **The vicious war** devastated both countries and killed 1.5 million people. Iraq launched deadly bombing raids and Iran replied with missile attacks on Baghdad.

- **In 1988,** careful negotiations by the UN leader Perez de Cuéllar arranged a peace settlement.

> ...**FASCINATING FACT**...
> No war has ever used chemical weapons
> more devastatingly than the Iran-Iraq War.

201

The break-up of the USSR

- **After Stalin died,** in 1953, many people were released from the Siberian prison camps, but the USSR, under its new leader Khrushchev, stayed restrictive and secretive.

- **The KGB** was a secret police force. It dealt harshly with anyone who did not toe the communist line.

- **In the 1980s,** cracks began to appear in the communist machine.

- **In 1985,** Mikhail Gorbachev became Soviet leader and introduced policies of *perestroika* (economic reform), *glasnost* (government openness) and *demokratizatsiya* (increased democracy).

- **Gorbachev** also made cuts in army spending and improved relationships with the West.

- **In 1989,** a McDonalds restaurant opened in Moscow.

- **As people** in the USSR gained freedom, so people in communist eastern Europe demanded freedom. New democratic governments were elected in Hungary, Poland, Czechoslovakia, Romania and Bulgaria.

- **The republics** within the USSR demanded independence too, and in 1991 the USSR was dissolved and replaced by a Commonwealth of Independent States (CIS).

- **Gorbachev's reforms** angered Communist Party leaders, who staged a coup and imprisoned Gorbachev, but he was freed and the coup was brought down by Boris Yeltsin, who became the first president of Russia (once the largest republic in the USSR).

◄ *Mikhail Gorbachev.*

- **Under Yeltsin,** the state industries of the Soviet era were gradually broken up and Russia seemed to be moving towards Western-style capitalism. But the collapse of the Communist Party structure led to chaos, lawlessness and economic problems. In 2000, the Russians elected Vladimir Putin as president, a strong leader who they hoped would see them out of the crisis.

▲ *The Kremlin, in Moscow, dates back to the 1100s and is a walled collection of palaces and churches. Home to the tsars, it then became the seat of USSR government.*

203

The European Union

- **The European Union** is an organization of 15 European countries, including France, Germany and the UK.

- **After World War 2** ended in 1945, Jean Monnet promoted the idea of uniting Europe economically and politically.

- **In 1952,** six countries formed the European Coal and Steel Community (ECSC), to trade in coal and steel.

- **The success of the ECSC** led the member countries to break down all trade barriers between them as part of the European Community (EC), in 1967.

- **1973-81:** six new countries join the EC, including the UK.

- **In 1992,** the 12 EC members signed a treaty at Maastricht in the Netherlands to form the European Union (EU).

- **The EU** added cooperation on justice and police matters and cooperation in foreign and security affairs to the economic links of the EC. These three links are called the 'Three Pillars' of the EU.

- **The EU** has four governing bodies: the Commission, Council of Ministers, Court of Justice and Parliament. The 17 Commissioners submit laws for the Council to make and put into effect. Parliament has very limited powers but is gaining more each year.

- **In 1999,** the EU launched the Euro, which is intended to become a single European currency.

▶ *The European Commission building in Strasbourg. The Parliament is in Brussels. The Court of Justice is in Luxembourg.*

Latin America

▶ *Activist Che Guevara played a major part in Cuba's revolution. Leaving Cuba for South America, he met an early death at the hands of political enemies and became an enduring hero, especially to young people in the 1960s and '70s.*

- **In the 1950s,** many Latin American governments sought to break their dependence on single farm products such as sugar and beef through major industrialization programmes.

- **'Populist' alliances** between workers and industrialists came to the fore.

- **In Argentina,** Juan Perón came to power and tried to build up industry at the expense of agriculture.

- **Landowners** suffering from the emphasis on industry began to form alliances with the army. Army coups took place in Argentina (1955), Brazil (1964) and Chile (1973).

- **Many** of the military regimes were secretly backed by foreign powers such as the USA.

- **In the 1960s,** some Latin American groups resorted to guerrilla warfare to bring down the military dictatorships.

- **In 1959,** an Argentinian communist called Che Guevara helped overthrow the dictator of Cuba and bring Fidel Castro to power.

- **In 1967,** Che Guevara was killed leading a guerilla band trying to overthrow the dictator of Bolivia.

- **Under the dictators,** opposition was suppressed and many people were tortured, imprisoned or 'disappeared', as 20,000 did in Argentina.

- **In the 1980s and 90s,** economic failure brought down most Latin American dictators, including Pinochet in Chile (1990) and Galtieri in Argentina (1983).

◀ *Eva Perón, also known as Evita (1919-52), was the wife of Argentinian leader Juan Perón. A former actress, she was loved by ordinary people and wielded great power in her husband's government.*

Index

Index

Index

Index

Index

Index

Index

Index

Acknowledgements

The publishers would like to thank the following artists
who have contributed to this book:

Peter Dennis, Nicholas Forder, Terry Gabbey, Studio Galante, Sally Holmes,
Richard Hook, Angus McBride, Terry Riley, Martin Sanders, Guy Smith,
Nick Spender, Rudi Vizi, Mike White

The publisher would like to thank the following sources for the use
of their photographs:

CORBIS: Page 13 Gianni Dagli; Page 33 Michael Maslan Historic Photographs;
Page 77 Philadelphia Museum of Art; Page 79 Asian Art and Archaeology Inc;
Page 93 Macduff Everton; Page 102 Leonard de Selva; Page128 Archivo
Iconografico, S.A.; Page156 Sean Sexton Collection; Page 175 Corbis;
Page 181 Angelo Hornak; Page 199 Bettmann

All other pictures from the Miles Kelly Archives